Housing Finance
A B A S I C G U I D E

HENRY AUGHTON

Shelter
NATIONAL CAMPAIGN FOR THE HOMELESS

Housing Finance
A Basic Guide

Henry Aughton

Second revised edition.
Published in November 1986 by Shelter, 157 Waterloo Road,
London SE1 8XF.
© Shelter

Typesetting by Boldface, 17&21 Clerkenwell Road, London EC1.
Cover design by Spencers, 1-5 Clerkenwell Road, London EC1.
Printed by RAP Ltd., 201 Spotland Road, Rochdale.

Trade distribution: Turnaround, 27 Horsell Road,
London N5   01-609 7836.

Cover photos: Paul Mattsson/Frame (estate agents), Rob Cowan
(Dulwich Gate), and Stuart McPherson/Shelter ('for sale' boards).

ISBN 0 901242 73X

The views expressed in this book are not necessarily Shelter policy.

Foreword

THIS BASIC GUIDE was first published in 1981, and the many important changes since then mean that an updated version is overdue. It is hoped that this second edition, taking in all significant developments up to early 1986, will be as useful as the first.

Its purpose is to describe the way that housing finance works in England and Wales in both the private and public sectors, whether property is rented, owned, or in the process of being purchased. It is not primarily intended for those seeking professional qualifications in the housing or finance fields – they will turn to the specialist texts which deal with the subject, though they may find it a useful beginning. Rather it is for councillors, those who work in housing departments, housing associations and advice centres, and those who are interested in the subject for other reasons.

The intention has been to avoid technical terms and jargon altogether, whilst giving the ordinary individual an understanding of the way that each of the main sectors works, and how each compares with the others, financially and socially. If this has been done, this small contribution to a large subject will have been well worthwhile, for lack of understanding of the main features of Britain's housing finance system is the rule rather than the exception, and it is this which allows misrepresentation and distortion of the real picture, especially in respect of the degree of help which different classes of householder receive from the public purse. It is also this lack of understanding which has meant that reform has been woefully neglected for so long.

Henry Aughton, November 1986

Note about the author

Henry Aughton has a background in both housing and finance. He was Hemel Hempstead's Borough Treasurer for 14 years and subsequently Dacorum District Council's first Chief Executive. Altogether, he has had 47 years' experience in local government. He was housing advisor to the Association of Municipal Corporations and specialist advisor in 1977 and 1978 to the House of Commons Environment Sub-Committee. He has also served on housing working parties of the Chartered Institute of Public Finance and Accountancy and is currently Honorary Treasurer of the National Housing and Town Planning Council, as well as Deputy Chairman of Shelter.

Contents

Introduction   1

Council housing   3

Housing Associations   25

Private rented sector   31

Housing Benefit   39

Owner occupied sector   49

Overview   61

Reform: what they say   73

Reform: the right was ahead   81

Index   93

Introduction

It ain't what people don't know that causes trouble.
It's what they know that ain't so.
MARK TWAIN (1835-1910)

THESE DAYS buying a house to live in is seen by many people as the norm. Just over 60 per cent of the population is in owner occupied housing – flats or houses either owned outright or being paid for with a mortgage. But this has not always been the case. Before the first world war most people rented from private landlords rather than owned their homes and there was no council housing. It was quite usual for even the better-off to rent rather than buy.

By the end of the first world war, though, the private rented sector had begun to decline sharply, as other more attractive avenues for investment opened up. In spite of demand, the supply of rented accommodation shrank year after year. Large numbers of dwellings were demolished as slums, and investment by landlords had become thoroughly unattractive. As costs went up but rents did not, few landlords missed the chance of selling to sitting tenants, or better still, selling with vacant possession when tenants left.

Other countries faced similar problems and many chose to give public funds to housing associations so that they could provide the extra rented housing needed. This country did not have an extensive ready-made housing association movement, however, and the job fell to local authorities. Councils were seen as the only bodies which could provide and manage, with financial help from central government, sufficient numbers of houses at rents within the means of ordinary working people. So began, with the Housing Act 1919, the provision of rented council housing. Today there are about six million council dwellings – about 28 per cent of the country's total housing stock.

Owning a house, on the other hand, became steadily more attractive. The growth of the building societies made ownership possible for many more people. And in 1963 tax advantages gave another boost to owner occupation – mortgage tax relief became an outright subsidy. Finally, the rapid inflation of the last 15 years, together with yet more tax advantages, made home ownership the most lucrative investment any ordinary person could ever make.

The enormous changes of the last 60 years show the overwhelming importance of the financial arrangements affecting housing. Yet our methods of financing housing are acknowledged almost universally to be in need of drastic reform. They give most help to those who need it least and far too little to those who need it most. As well as being inequitable, the soaring cost, and the way investment is diverted into housing and away from other sectors, is a source of the greatest concern right across the political spectrum.

To come to any sensible conclusions on the way housing finance should be reformed, it is essential to grasp how it works now. The following chapters deal with the way different sectors of housing are financed before drawing comparisons and setting out the arguments for reform.

Council housing

Providing the houses

HOUSES ARE built on borrowed money. An individual buys or builds with the help of a loan, usually from a building society or a bank, paid back with interest over a period probably of 25 years. A council also finances the building of houses through loans, but repayment is over 60 years – the assumed life of a house.

Governments invariably set down the period within which any loans raised by a council must be repaid. Although councils can repay over a shorter time if they want to, most go for the longest period available. They are anxious to keep loan charges – interest on the loans plus an element of repayment – down to a minimum.

Repayment is by what is called the sinking fund method, a formula which means a very small repayment in the first year, and in each succeeding year the sum to be repaid is worked out by adding five per cent to the previous year's payment. The starting point is calculated so that by the sixtieth year the whole loan will have been repaid. Interest on the outstanding loan decreases a little each year, since it is payable on a declining total amount. It is rather like the annuity method used with building society mortgage loans – principal repayments gradually increase, interest payments gradually decline.

In providing houses, it is necessary to incur expenditure on land, roads, sewers, and of course the buildings themselves. The expenditure on the acquisition of these permanent assets is called capital expenditure. The transactions involved are recorded in a housing capital account, showing on the expenditure side what has been spent on land, roads, sewers and construction, and on the income side the loans raised to finance the operation, and any capital receipts (money raised by the sale of houses and land) which have been used for capital expenditure.

Where the money comes from

A council has many services besides housing which require loans to finance capital expenditure. Instead of letting each service raise its own loans, it has a loans fund, which raises money from individuals, financial institutions and the government's Public Works Loan Board. The loans fund acts as lender to whichever department needs a loan to finance capital spending; and so each service – housing in this case – has only one lender to deal with, the loans fund. This is a great accounting and administrative convenience, and has other important advantages.

The loans fund borrows most of its money for fixed terms of two, three or more years, even up to 60 years. It will have only a very small proportion of 'temporary' money, which has to be repaid at short notice. Like a building society, it needs to re-borrow when repayments have to be made to lenders; but unlike a building society there is no question of rapid withdrawals if, for example, other forms of investment become more attractive because of interest rate changes. The precise amount of each year's repayments is known well in advance.

The loans fund has to pay interest, of course, to all those from whom it has borrowed, and it charges this interest, at an average rate, to all the services which owe it money. Each year, then, it gets back from each of the services (housing, parks, education, etc.) the interest on the loans and an appropriate amount of repayment of principal.

Government control of capital spending

It seems rather difficult to believe these days, but until 1976 there was no restriction on the number of houses any council chose to build. There was control over the costs of each individual scheme – councils had to show that building costs complied with the government's cost yardstick. If they did not, consent to borrow, called loan sanction, would be refused. But so long as costs did comply, a council could have as many schemes and build as many houses as it thought fit.

After 1976 the government took control over the number of housing units which councils could provide. There was a further change in 1978: loan sanctions were no longer required. Instead each council had to produce a Local Housing Strategy, setting out the need in its area for new council building, repairs and modernisation of older council dwellings, improvement grants for home owners, and loans for housing associations and home owners wanting to buy or repair properties. On the basis of this strategy it would then draw up each year a Housing Investment Programme (HIP), showing what it planned to spend on the items covered by its housing strategy. Both the strategy and the housing investment programme were to be submitted to the Department of the Environment, which would then grant permission to each council to borrow a total sum, to be spent on the items outlined in the council's HIP.

The different borrowing limits allocated to each council were supposed to reflect their differing needs for housing investment, while the total limit for borrowing by all councils was supposed to represent what the country could afford to spend.

The new HIP system was at first well received. The work connected with individual loan sanction applications would be avoided, a simpler method of cost control than the cost yardstick was promised, the common sense of local strategy planning was obvious. There was, however, another aspect which had doubtless occurred to central government but was not fully appreciated by local councils. This was the unprecedented degree of control which central government would henceforth exercise over local authority housing provision.

This was first brought home to councils in February 1980 when the government announced a £1,000 million cut in borrowing permission – just six weeks before the financial year was about to begin. Many councils were already committed to spending money on building contracts and could not reduce their expenditure so quickly; the government therefore went a stage further in the autumn of 1980 and banned all new building work until the following April. The result was a massive disruption of councils' strategies and investment programmes for the next two years – the very opposite of the smooth process of steady investment that HIPs were supposed to produce.

The government then created additional problems for councils by further reducing their borrowing permission but allowing them to use a prescribed proportion of capital receipts – money received from the sale of houses and land.

At first councils had no idea how much extra these capital receipts would allow them to spend, so they made underestimates to be on the safe side. As a result investment fell still further as councils spent less than they were actually allowed. By the autumn of 1982 even the prime minister Mrs Thatcher was urging councils to 'spend, spend, spend' on housing.

Since then, the proportion of capital receipts which councils are permitted to use to increase their borrowing limit has been steadily reduced: from 50 per cent to 40 per cent, and then to 20 per cent. But within their overall borrowing limit councils have been free to invest in what they see as the local priorities – this, of course, being one underlying principle of the housing investment programme idea. Even this, however, is being changed. In 1986-7 the government held back £50 million of loan sanction in order to give extra cash to councils which were following its policy of selling council housing estates to private developers. This procedure, called 'top-slicing' is clearly another step towards overall central government control of the housing programme. There is now no cost yardstick. Instead the Department of the Environment (DoE) looks at individual construction schemes at land acquisition stage rather than when a detailed scheme with estimated costs has been prepared. In cases where the DoE considers that there will be 'exceptionally poor value', subsidy will be refused on the whole scheme, if, that is, the council is eligible for subsidy; nowadays most are not.

At the time of writing, the government has recently published a green paper on local authority finance, *Paying for Local Government*. Its most notorious proposal is for the abolition of domestic rates, which are to be replaced by a poll tax. But it also contains many other proposals for changes to local authority finance, including new arrangements for the control of capital expenditure. Two ideas are put forward: one for a system of external borrowing limits, the other for a system more like the present with more control over gross expenditure.

The government has indicated that it wants to change the arrangements for local authority capital expenditure fairly quickly – within the next year or so. At the same time, the Labour Party has also proposed reform – in its case the lifting of central government capital controls, with expenditure being determined by local decisions, influenced (presumably) by central government subsidy arrangements. For local government, the uncertainty about capital investment in housing looks set to continue for some years to come.

When the houses have been provided

On the completion of a scheme, capital expenditure on land, roads, sewers and buildings ceases. But from then on there will be continuing spending on management, maintenance, loan interest, and debt redemption. This recurring revenue expenditure is met out of the rents charged to tenants, government subsidies if there is entitlement to them, mortgage interest where tenants have bought their homes and raised a mortgage from the council, and interest on capital receipts where tenants buy but obtain a mortgage from other sources. There may also be contributions from the rates.

These annual transactions are recorded in a housing revenue account (HRA), which every housing authority must keep in a form prescribed by the Department of the Environment.

The housing revenue account

A typical housing revenue account (HRA) of a medium-sized district council outside London is shown on p.8. The accounts of London boroughs take exactly the same form, but the figures are much larger, since most of them provide housing on a large scale, and the costs are very much higher. In most inner London boroughs there would also be very large contributions from the rates. Although rents and government subsidies in London are higher, costs are so much higher still that most London councils feel that heavy rate fund contributions are unavoidable. The alternative would be unacceptably high rents.

The housing revenue account is entirely separate from the council's general rate fund revenue account, which covers services other than housing. Before the Housing Act 1980, housing authorities were required to operate on a 'break-even' basis, and could not carry forward surpluses except in respect of a reasonable working balance. This was known as the no-profit rule. Now surpluses may be carried forward or transferred to the general rate fund; but if there is going to be a deficit, a rate fund contribution sufficient to keep the account in balance must be made. So although a surplus may be carried forward, a deficit may not.

HOUSING REVENUE ACCOUNT
Year ended 31 March 1985

	£000	£000
Expenditure:		
Loan charges – principal	1,049	
interest	8,384	9,433
Capital expenditure met from revenue		
Supervision and management – general	2,249	
special	1,061	3,310
Repairs and maintenance		4,515
Administrative costs of debt management		57
Other expenditure		–
Transfer to General Rate Fund		–
Working balance at year end		438
		17,753
Income:		
Working balance at beginning of year		1,140
Net rent income (excluding rates etc)	6,605	
Standard amount rent rebates	1,840	
Rebates in excess of standard	–	
Certificated amount rent rebates	5,640	
Total gross rents		14,085
Other rents and income		356
Housing subsidies under Housing Act 1980		–
Interest on sales of council houses		2,080
Rate fund contributions –		
Cost of administering rent rebate scheme	88	
Other (excluding those associated with rent rebates)	4	92
		17,753

Items shown in the housing revenue account

Loan charges consist of interest on the outstanding loan debt, and repayment of a proportion of the principal.

Capital expenditure met from revenue is items of a capital nature for which a loan is not raised. These may be small items which are not considered to be worth borrowing for. Or, frequently, they will cover expenditure not accepted by the Department of the Environment for loan purposes, such as architectural and other costs which are in excess of prescribed limits, or are incurred on abortive schemes.

Supervision and management is divided into two categories. 'General' expenditure includes normal management costs, largely salaries for management, rent collection, administration of the waiting list, and advisory services (if any). It also includes central administration charges for work done by the legal and finance departments. 'Special' expenditure includes those costs which do not apply to all the housing stock, such as caretaking, cleaning, lighting, maintenance of lifts, stairways and common areas in flats, and similar costs for sheltered accommodation for elderly people, and sometimes estate and playground upkeep. Where blocks of flats have refuse chutes or other special arrangements, some councils charge the cost of refuse collection from such premises to HRA 'special supervision', unaware, apparently, that this means that council tenants are paying twice for refuse collection, since they pay rates like everyone else.

Repairs and maintenance covers expenditure on maintenance of the housing stock. Usually it is the actual amount spent in the year of account, but some councils keep a separate housing repairs account, charge the cost of repairs to it, and make an annual contribution to it from the parent HRA. The idea is to avoid big fluctuations in repair costs from year to year and to build up a fund for exceptionally large items, such as when say a whole estate needs re-wiring, or when costly structural repairs have to be made.

But most councils prefer to borrow for major repair expenditure items, rather than use a repair account. This means more on the loan charges item, less on the repairs.

Net rent income: the council collects an 'inclusive' rent from each tenant, covering both rent and rates. This is what the tenant regards as the rent. But the rates element is not rent at all, of course, and goes straight to the council's rating account. The housing department is in effect acting as rate collector for the council. Only the rent element goes to the HRA.

Some tenants can afford to pay the rent in full; those whose incomes are not high enough, according to DHSS scales, to enable them to do this are entitled to housing benefits in the form of rent rebates, which result in rent reductions. All rent payments, whether in full or reduced by rebates, make up the net rent income.

Rent rebates: the next three items are contributions to the HRA which make good the rent income lost by the granting of rebates.

★ Standard rebates replace the former rent rebates which councils gave before 1983 except where tenants were in receipt of supplementary benefits from the DHSS. Ninety per cent of the cost is met by government grant, the other ten per cent by rate fund contributions.

★ Excess rebates are additional help where the council chooses to be more generous than the national scales. All the cost falls on the rates.

★ Certificated rebates are those taken over from the DHSS in 1983, and are met wholly by government grant.

The housing benefit scheme, intended to simplify previous arrangements, has suffered repeated changes since it was introduced, and has resulted in hideous complexity. It is dealt with more fully in Chapter 4.

Other rents and income is mainly made up of rents from garages, land not yet developed, and shops – where the council has provided shops as part of an estate development.

Housing subsidies under the Housing Act 1980 is self-explanatory. Before 1980 this was a large item in every HRA, usually meeting 30 per cent or more of the expenditure. Now, however, most councils outside London, like the one shown here, no longer receive any housing subsidy from central government.

Interest on sales of council houses comes from two sources, according to whether tenants, in exercising their 'right to buy', raise a mortgage loan from the council or another source.

Where purchasers go to a building society or other lending institution the council receives the full sales proceeds at once from the lender. As these are capital receipts (since they result from the sale of capital assets) they may only be used for further capital expenditure, or for debt redemption. But as government restrictions mean that only a small proportion (at present 20 per cent) of capital receipts can be spent in any year, most will be invested for the time being. The interest on such investments goes to the HRA, and accounts for most of this item.

Where tenants raise mortgages from the council, receipt of the proceeds spreads over the whole mortgage period, as purchasers make periodic repayments of principal and interest. Only the interest goes to the HRA, and this makes up the rest of this item. The principal repayment element is a capital receipt, and may not be paid into the HRA. It can be added to the other capital receipts, or may go at once to debt redemption.

Rate fund contributions: the first item is the contribution which every council must make to meet the cost of administering the rent rebate scheme, so far as it is not covered by government grant.

The second item, 'other rate fund contributions', is made up of any other contributions from the rates. These may be compulsory, if needed to avoid a deficit; or may be voluntary, either to avoid unacceptably high rent increases, or to meet expenditure charged to the HRA which, in the council's view, should be borne by the whole community.

As noted earlier, some rate fund contributions are included in two of the rent rebate items – standard amount rebates, where the rates bear ten per cent of the cost, and excess rebates, which are wholly borne by the rates.

A point to note about exchequer grants

So far as council housing is concerned, there are two kinds of payments by the exchequer which affect the HRA. The first is housing subsidies under the Housing Act 1980. None have been received in the HRA illustrated here, and as noted earlier, few councils outside London still receive them. Where they are received, they benefit all tenants by meeting part of housing costs, thus reducing the level of rent income that is required.

The second kind is rent rebate subsidies, and they are not shown in the HRA as separate items. They constitute 90 per cent of the £1,840,000 standard rent rebates item, the other ten per cent being met by rate fund contributions; and they make up the whole of the £5,640,000 certificated rent rebates, those which used to be the responsibility of the DHSS, now dealt with by the council but fully covered by Exchequer subsidy. (To be strictly accurate, the entitlement is 100.6 per cent of the certificated rebates, as an acknowledgement that their administration involves the council in extra cost.)

Government representatives often refer to rent rebate subsidies as if they were housing subsidies, which is incorrect. The only sensible course is to distinguish between housing subsidies, which affect rent levels, and rent rebate subsidies, which do not, for rebates operate after rent levels have been set, and are income support, relief of poverty, not housing subsidies at all.

Subsidies for council housing

Under the Housing Act 1919, councils were expected to charge rents which were similar to those of comparable rented property in the area. Government subsidy was payable to bridge the gap between outgoings (debt charges, repairs, management) and rent income. Only a very modest contribution had to be made from the rates.

The system frightened the Treasury out of its wits because of its open-ended nature and the 1919 Act provisions were scrapped within three years. No more was heard of deficiency subsidies for over 50 years.

Successive Housing Acts were passed every few years, always accepting the first principle that subsidies existed so that houses could be provided at rents ordinary working people could pay. Treasury fears of an open-ended commitment were stilled by stipulating that the government would pay a fixed annual lump sum for each dwelling, with the local authority making a compulsory contribution from the rates. (This obligation ended in 1956, although many councils continued to make contributions to the HRA from the rate funds.) But this system made no allowance for regional cost differences and there was no provision for withdrawal or alteration if conditions changed, as, of course, they did. Instead, the government of the day would then bring in a new Housing Act, specifying subsidies appropriate to the new situation, but not making any alteration to subsidy entitlement on earlier schemes.

This went on until 1967, when a more sophisticated version of the same thing was introduced. The 1967 Act subsidy gave more help where

capital costs were high, less where they were low and it insulated housing provision from unduly high interest rates. This system produced a
lot of houses and lasted until 1972 in spite, once again, of intense Treasury
dislike.

Everything changed with the Conservative government's Housing
Finance Act 1972. It marked the end of the consensus in housing,
removing the freedom of local councils to fix rents and obliging them to
move rapidly to much higher fair rents similar to those applying in part
of the private rented sector. Existing subsidies, which authorities had
thought were inviolable, were to be rapidly withdrawn and replaced by a
new type of subsidy, a straightforward deficiency subsidy, though that
description was tactfully avoided. The Act called it a rising costs subsidy.

The idea was that as existing subsidies were withdrawn, the lost income
would be more than covered by compulsory rent increases. These
increases would also be large enough to carry at least part of the rises in
costs which by 1972 were beginning to arouse misgivings, as inflation
started to accelerate. Indeed in many areas such steep rent increases (as
they then were) would actually produce surpluses, and where this happened the government would take a share of the surplus. But where the
rent increases did not cover the phased withdrawal of subsidies and any
increase in costs, the new rising costs subsidy would meet a large proportion of any shortfall.

This was reform with a vengeance, arousing sharper controversy than
at any time since councils had become involved with housing. The first
act of the incoming Labour government in 1974 was to repeal the fair
rent provision for council housing and replace the rising costs subsidy
by yet another, this time temporary, version. This was a contribution
equal to 66 per cent of the loan charges on all borrowing after March
1975, together with a continuation of whatever previous subsidies
remained at 31 March 1975 under the 1972 Act. Freedom in rent fixing
was also restored to councils.

All these were intended as stop-gap measures pending a complete
overhaul of housing finance which would follow a comprehensive review
set in train by the Environment Minister, Anthony Crosland. He had
made clear in a number of excellent speeches his understanding of the
existing anomalies and inequities, and his commitment to reform. But
he was moved to the Foreign Office just as the review got under way,

and the result, a consultation document, *Housing Policy* (Cmnd. 6851), when it finally appeared in 1977, was a sorry let-down after the high hopes of a couple of years earlier.

The whole purpose of the review had been to deal with housing finance in all its aspects, and so avoid what Crosland had described as the main fault of the 1972 Act, its treatment of council housing in isolation. Yet in the event, the private rented sector was left for a separate committee to look at; the owner occupied sector was regarded as not in need of any reform; housing associations were not mentioned except for a comment that the subsidies proposed for council housing could also be applied to them; and proposals for reform of council housing were again being made in isolation.

The main proposals of the 1977 consultation document were for a local housing strategy in each housing authority area, a housing investment programme based on that local strategy (already described earlier), a tenants' charter, and a new subsidy system. This last was yet another version of a deficiency subsidy. Subsidies already being paid under earlier housing acts would continue. Housing costs would of course go on rising. Rent income would also rise, in line with earnings. And insofar as the increases were not covered by rising rent income and rate aid, the new subsidy would meet any shortfall.

The starting point – existing rents, existing rate burden, existing subsidies – meant that existing inequalities would remain as part of the system. Central government control would be greatly strengthened, since the secretary of state would have the final say in what should count as acceptable cost increases, and even more important, what rent increases should be assumed for subsidy calculation purposes. However, there was always the safeguard that rents would not rise faster than earnings. But before the new system could be put into effect the Labour government was replaced by the 1979 Conservative government.

The new subsidy system

The new secretary of state, Michael Heseltine, took on the Labour government's proposed new subsidy system with enthusiasm. It gave him everything he could possibly want to obtain massive reductions in subsidies to the public rented sector. The only change he needed to make before including it in the Housing Act 1980, was to exclude the linking of rent increases with increased earnings.

The new system provided that, as in Labour's proposals, the starting point would be existing subsidies, rents and rate fund contributions. The new subsidy would consist of the 'base amount', which was the total subsidy payable in the preceding year, plus the 'housing costs differential', which is the increase in the total reckonable housing costs over those for the preceding year. From this total is deducted the 'local contribution differential' – the extra amount the government expects the local council to pay towards housing through increased rents or rate fund contributions.

The local contribution differential is popularly expressed in terms of an increase in the average weekly rent. The government assumes that average rents will rise by the prescribed amount, although councils could choose to make smaller rent increases and make up the difference from the rates. The formula *base amount plus housing costs differential minus local contribution differential* thus provides for a straightforward deficiency subsidy to meet cost increases which cannot be covered by increased rents or rate fund contributions. As applied by Mr Heseltine, however, it became the perfect formula for reducing subsidies – in fact for discontinuing them altogether for many authorities.

Heseltine's strategy was to secure rent increases much greater than increases in earnings because, he contended, the proportion of housing costs borne by unrebated rents had been falling steadily in recent years, and this trend had to be reversed. Even before the Act reached the statute book he issued what he called 'guidelines' (since he did not yet have the power to require rent increases) for two rent rises of £1.50 and 60p in the financial year 1980/81. And when the Act came into force he specified further average rent increases for 1981/2 of £3.25 and for 1982/3 of £2.50. In three years rents more than doubled. And still further rent increases were prescribed, though not at quite the formidable rate as previously. For one thing, when enormous rent increases resulted in a council no longer being eligible for subsidy, it was not quite so easy to compel it to make further rent increases for which there was no justification.

As part of the new system the minister has the power to prescribe for groups of authorities, and even individual authorities, what he regards as reasonable levels of expenditure on repairs and on supervision. The effects on standards of maintenance and management are far-reaching. In settling the housing subsidy for each local authority the minister assumes that his directions for rent increases and his decisions about admissible levels of expenditure on repairs and management have been followed. If they haven't, any expenditure which does not comply with the minister's criteria will not qualify for subsidy.

This system gives the secretary of state a very powerful lever for coercing councils into obeying government directions. For sixty years, save for Peter Walker's Housing Finance Act 1972 with its brief two year life (when councils lost their feedom to fix their own rents and were required to move towards 'fair' rents), councils had had complete freedom in rent-fixing, in the amount of support provided from the rates, and what was spent on repairs and management. The government had always decided what level of subsidy would encourage building for rent, but it had then left councils to build or not, to set their own rent levels, and to decide how much support, if any, was needed from the rates. The only constraint was that they must keep the housing revenue account in balance.

Now all was changed. The purpose of subsidies was no longer to encourage building, but to give the government the means whereby rent policy would be obliged to follow the government's so-called 'guidelines'. But this was not the end of it. When a council no longer receives subsidies, it has no incentive to follow a government directive to do something it sees no need to do. Some other form of compulsion is required, and the Local Government, Planning and Land Act 1980, on the face of it nothing to do with housing, provided it.

This Act introduced a new way of distributing rate support grant (RSG), which meets a proportion of non-housing expenditure (a large proportion in the case of the metropolitan district councils). The distribution of RSG was to be by a new very detailed and complicated formula, grant related expenditure assessment (GREA) which would establish for each authority the level of expenditure it needed to enable it to provide standard levels of service for virtually everything it did. And RSG would be distributed in accordance with this new magic formula. There would be fair treatment for all, help where help was needed and no unnecessary help where it was not needed.

The reality was very different. The formula is of unbelievable complexity and is generally considered by everyone outside Whitehall to be ludicrously inadequate for its stated purpose. So far as housing is concerned, the first year's figures included a factor (E.7) which purported to take account of regional rent levels and penalised authorities which charged less than these by reducing their RSG entitlement. Some authorities even found themselves penalised for the vigour with which they had promoted council house sales in response to government exhortations. These being profitable in the early years meant they had not needed to raise rents by as much as their less diligent neighbours. Now they were being punished for not doing something they had no need to do and which, in fact, would have been illegal before 1980, since up to that date the law required them to operate on a 'break-even' basis. They were not pleased; and the use of E.7 was quietly discontinued. It can, however, be reintroduced whenever the minister thinks fit.

Fixing rents

While there can be big differences in council rents in different parts of the country, there is relative uniformity within each authority's area and a logical relationship between the rents of different properties. This is because of rent pooling.

Until the 1930s, when a council completed a housing scheme it would calculate the loan charges on the capital spending, add likely costs for repairs and management, and deduct the subsidy it had been promised. The result gave the rent income which the scheme needed to produce. Some contribution from rates might be necessary if rents looked like being too far out of line. Because rents were set for each individual scheme as it was completed, not surprisingly, councils soon found themselves with schemes of perhaps identical houses which were being let at significantly different rents.

Since two identical houses must be worth the same rent, something had to be wrong were this not the case. By the 1930s, the more progressive councils accepted that the logical way of fixing rents was to cease looking at the housing stock scheme by scheme, and to look at the lot. So they did for the whole housing stock what they had been doing for each individual scheme – they looked at the total loan charges and the cost of maintaining and managing the whole stock, calculated how far government subsidies (and perhaps some rate aid) would go towards meeting total outgoings, and calculated necessary rent income according to the balance not met by subsidy.

Having settled what total rent income was needed, a council had next to decide on the rent of individual houses or flats. It would aim to produce a rent structure in which the rent of any property would be seen as fair when compared with the rent of any other property, taking into account size, location and amenities. Now this may sound a formidable task, but in fact it is nothing of the kind. Every dwelling is already assessed for rating purposes with a gross value and a rateable value (which is gross value less an allowance for repairs). The gross value is supposed to represent the annual rent which a landlord would expect to receive. The figures are always out of date because of delays in revaluation but their relativity, one property with another, is not far off the mark, and they offer a ready-made basis of comparison, since they reflect size and quality. Many councils, perhaps most, look no further; others seek greater refinement by some formula of their own.

If gross value is the chosen basis, all the council has to do is to take net outgoings of say £12m (total outgoings of say £14m less subsidies £2m), and relate that to the total gross value of the housing stock. Suppose total gross value is £8m, then rents of one and a half times gross value will produce the required £12m rent income. This will not only be correct in total, it will also be reasonably correct for each individual dwelling, unless there is something very wrong with the gross value of any of them which is unlikely, and even less likely to be overlooked by the rating and housing departments.

The acceptance of rent pooling as the only sensible way of dealing with the problem of varying capital costs (and subsidies) of very similar houses spread quickly, and became universal in the years following the second world war. But the system applies only within the area of each housing authority, and consequently neighbouring councils may have differing rent levels for no other reason than historic accident (such as whether they have a small or large proportion of earlier low-cost houses) or the size of their current building programme. Where this happens, there is an anomaly, as there is wherever a council gives significantly more help out of rates than its neighbours in order to avoid unacceptably high rent levels.

When councils were free to settle their own rent levels, the need for an increase to meet increasing costs would usually be met by a decision to raise all rents by an average weekly amount, and this would be secured by smaller increases for some properties, larger for others, keeping the relativity of one property with another which already existed. With the massive rent increases imposed in the 1980s there has probably been some departure from previous practice, with flat-rate increases of the amounts prescribed by the minister's guidelines in many areas, rather than proportionate increases.

The sale of council houses

As well as the new subsidy system the Housing Act 1980 also contained the *Right to Buy* scheme, in fulfilment of the Conservative Party's election manifesto pledge to give council tenants the right to buy their houses at a discount.

The right to buy applied to any tenant whose tenancy had been in existence for three years or more, except for dwellings designed or specially adapted for old people. This has now been reduced to two years, at which point a tenant has the right to purchase at market value less a discount of 32 per cent, and for every extra year's tenancy there is a further one per cent discount, up to a maximum of 60 per cent (80 per cent for flats). The selling price may not be less than the cost to the council of providing the house. Older houses, where the cost was low, would undoubtedly qualify for full discount appropriate to the length of tenancy; but on recently built houses, which cost a great deal, there could be little or no discount.

As well as the right to buy there is also a right to a council mortgage for anyone who does buy, unless the tenant prefers, and is able, to get a mortgage elsewhere.

A building society's lending criteria (size of loan in relation to the householder's income, percentage of purchase price which can be borrowed, length of mortgage with older purchasers) are likely to be less favourable than with a council mortgage. One hundred per cent mortgages – which some purchasers might need – are rare indeed with building societies. Furthermore, an applicant for a council mortgage can include earning members of the family in a joint application.

On the other hand, when it comes to interest rates the advantage lies with the building societies, for a council is required to charge the recommended building society rate, or its own average loans pool rate plus ¼ per cent, whichever is the higher. As a result a substantial proportion of sales are being financed by building societies.

There are other facilities. A tenant who, because of insufficient income, cannot meet the conditions for a council mortgage of the amount needed has the right to put down £100 for the option to purchase within the following two years. The price of the house will remained fixed at the original level. If the tenant can afford to buy within the two years, the £100 comes off the purchase price. If he decides not to go ahead, the £100 is refunded. Alternatively, a tenant who cannot afford to buy outright can buy part of the dwelling under a shared ownership scheme.

Detailed requirements are laid down by the Housing Act 1980 as to the steps a council must take when any tenant gives notice of intention to exercise the right to buy. These are designed to ensure that lack of enthusiasm on the part of the council shall not adversely affect the tenant's position.

There is no doubt that the right to buy scheme was immensely popular and an unqualified success for the government from an electoral point of view. The financial advantages for those tenants who can afford to buy are obvious – no problem about raising a mortgage if the repayments can be met, the chance to become a home-owner at perhaps as little as 40 per cent of the true value of the home, deliverance from future steep and unending rent increases, and an opportunity to acquire personal wealth such as the ordinary tenant had never dreamed of. The tenant would be helping her or himself, and was told they would be helping their less fortunate neighbours at the same time, for it was claimed that since sales would be profitable, even at large discounts, the remaining tenants and the ratepayers would also benefit.

Tenants who wished to buy were naturally enthusiastic about the new right, and those who could not afford to take advantage of the scheme were almost as enthusiastic; their chance might come, and in the meantime they did not begrudge the good fortune of those neighbours who were in a position to buy.

There was another side to the picture, seldom mentioned at the time, in spite of the valiant efforts of *Shelter* and a handful of others concerned with housing problems. Apart from the financial effects, looked at in more detail in the next section, there are also the social consequences. The housing problem in this country is mainly one of a shortage of rented accommodation of reasonable standard at rents which ordinary people can afford to pay. Selling rented property obviously reduces the stock of rented accommodation. From three to four per cent of a council's total stock becomes vacant each year (from moves out of the district or into private ownership, or through deaths) providing an important supply of re-lets for the accommodation of people in housing need – indeed the only source, where the housing authority is not building. A smaller stock means fewer re-lets. Massive cuts in council building at the same time as a drive to persuade sitting tenants to buy cannot but have the most serious effects on the prospects of those who must rent.

Sales also reduce the average quality of the remaining stock; it is the best houses which are sold; people do not buy flats in tower blocks. Transfers to more suitable property will be fewer. Waiting lists will lengthen.

The policy of selling at large discounts will eventually come to be seen as a bizarre and damaging aberration, benefiting an already well-housed minority, to the detriment of the rest. It is an extraordinary state of affairs when those who have bought at the high market prices of recent years, praised for their determination to stand on their own two feet, and those who would like to buy but cannot afford to, can see some council tenants (whom they have been told are unnecessarily subsidised anyway), being given another enormous subsidy by way of a price reduction to persuade them, too, to become home-owners. And can regard this as a praise-worthy advance in housing policy.

Financial effects of sales

No-one disputes the advantages of the right to buy scheme to most pur-chasers. Although mortgage repayments will at first be much heavier than paying rent, there are long-term benefits, for whilst rents go up every year, the mortgage payments will only rise if the interest rate goes up; and it is just as likely to come down. Mortgage payments also come to an end eventually, and the owner leaves a valuable property to his suc-cessors, whereas the tenant pays rent up to the end, and then leaves only a rent book to those who succeed him.

But the advantages of sales for the council – and therefore the taxpayer – are a matter of some controversy. Because the selling price, despite the large discount, will generally still be much more than the outstanding debt on the house sold, it was argued that selling could not fail to be profitable. This is like saying that someone who owns a house worth £30,000 and has paid off the mortgage, is making £10,000 profit if it is sold for £10,000. Such a person is, of course, making a loss of £20,000.

A financial appraisal of the effect of sales was, in fact, produced for the Labour government in 1977, but was not published. It showed sales as resulting in profits to councils in the early years after a sale, turning into substantial losses in later years. A second paper, done for the Conservative government in 1980 (presumably by the same civil servants – with admirable flexibility of mind) showed continuing profits.

The difference resulted from the different assumptions made about future subsidies, costs, and rent increases. A study carried out for the House of Commons Environment Select Committee and published in 1981, found that some of the assumptions which enabled the second paper to portray sales as yielding a profit were totally unrealistic. The study calculated that, in fact, the long term losses on council house sales, calculated over a 50 year period, were likely to average £12,500 per dwelling – so the 700,000 homes sold between 1980 and 1985 would mean an eventual loss of around £9,000 million (at mid-1980s prices). Yet even these calculations did not allow for the enormous rent increases and steep reductions in subsidies which have actually occurred since 1981. Nowadays we do not hear so much about the 'profitability' of selling council housing.

Sales financed by a council mortgage produce
★ a saving on repairs costs;
★ perhaps some saving on management costs; and
★ the receipt of mortgage interest on the outstanding loan.

The savings reduce the expenditure charged to the housing revenue account. The mortgage interest element of the repayment is credited to the income side of the HRA.

There will also be the repayment of principal, very little in the early years, more in later years. But this will not be brought into the HRA as income, since it is a capital receipt. It will be used to reduce the council's housing loan debt, or be added to other housing capital receipts and invested or used for capital spending.

If the purchase is financed by a mortgage from another source, the transactions differ somewhat. There will be no annual receipt of mortgage repayments, for these will be made to the lending institution. Instead, the council will receive the whole of the sale price at once, and if this is used for debt reduction, the loan charges to the HRA will be less; if it is invested, there will be investment income; or if it is used for new capital expenditure, the HRA will benefit by having less loan charges to bear than if the council had borrowed to finance the capital expenditure.

The HRA gains by the above items. Against this there are losses:
★ rent income is no longer received; and
★ exchequer subsidy, if still payable, will cease on the house being sold.

At first, then, since there is a saving on repairs, and since mortgage repayments (or income from invested capital receipts) is much greater than the previous rent, it will look as if selling is very profitable. That indeed is what is happening now, as we are in the early stages of all sales made so far under the right to buy scheme.

But this situation does not last. Mortgage repayments do not change (unless the interest rate changes), whereas rents, if the house had not been sold, would have gone up every year, and on the experience of the last four years would have gone up very steeply. A cross-over point will inevitably be reached in a few years when gains turn into losses, as councils find that the mortgage repayments they are receiving are far less than the rents would have been if houses had not been sold.

There is another consideration. Houses to rent are still going to be needed. It is inconceivable that council house building can continue for long at today's disastrously low rates of building. So it is difficult to see what economic sense there can be in selling houses at a fraction of the cost of building new ones to replace them.

Another sleight of hand is the claim that the Department of the Environment (DoE) is generously allowing councils to supplement their Housing Investment Programme (HIP) allocations (i.e. their borrowing permission for housing capital expenditure) by the use of part of their capital receipts from sales. Until 1980 a council had the right to use the *full* proceeds of any sale of a capital asset for other capital purposes, at a time to suit themselves. Ministry permission was required, but this was a formality; after all, it was their own money, resulting from the sale of their own property.

Now they were told that they would be allowed to spend up to 50 per cent of their accumulated capital receipts in any year, as if this was a generous concession, rather than a new restraint. This has since been reduced to 20 per cent.

Here they are, with six thousand million pounds in unspent capital receipt from sales lying in the bank; while borrowing permission under the HIP system has been reduced year after year; and facing the need for enormous expenditure on structural defects, disrepair, and much needed modernisation. The Association of Metropolitan Authorities estimates the cost of all this at £19 billion for England alone, and the Audit Commission confirms this and points to a backlog of work which is increasing the total at the rate of £1 billion a year. Yet we are asked to believe that it is necessary to curtail the spending of these capital receipts, lest it distort the economy (with 400,000 building trade workers out of work!).

There was a further discreditable twist to all this. The DoE, whilst stressing the financial advantages to councils of selling, appropriated part of the immediate apparent profits by reducing housing subsidies by half the surplus which arises from council house sales. It justified this by the remarkable argument that the government should be entitled to share in the profits because of the contributions (that is, housing subsidies) it made in the past. But it neglected to mention that those 'contributions' for which it now wants credit are considerably less than the cost of tax relief on mortgage interest would have been had the houses been privately owned. Nor does it propose to take half the losses when they arise, as they surely will. Nor does it explain how it arrives at 50 per cent as the appropriate share.

There is no rest for the wicked, however, and now that subsidies are payable to only a handful of councils outside London, this particular piece of sharp practice has lost much of its appeal.

Housing Associations

LONG BEFORE councils became involved in the provision of rented housing there were housing associations providing dwellings at modest rents, often established with the aid of charitable money from wealthy benefactors. The Peabody, Guinness, and Sutton Dwellings Trusts are three well-known examples.

The movement spread and government subsidies similar to those paid to local authorities became available. New kinds of organisation were tried – cost-rent, co-ownership, co-operative, self-build; but by far the major provision was still by conventional associations of dwellings for rent for those in need. However, the total stock, some 250,000 dwellings by 1970, was small compared to the 5 million or so then provided by councils.

The 1970-74 Conservative government decided upon a great expansion of the housing association movement, as a supplement (or perhaps as an alternative) to council housing. The Housing Corporation, already set up in 1964 to encourage the formation of cost-rent and co-ownership societies, was chosen as the main agent, with the task of encouraging the formation of housing associations to provide rented accommodation at fair rents. The Corporation would have an important supervisory responsibility, and would examine and approve schemes, and the government would provide the necessary financial support.

A bill to provide the relevant powers was drafted, but before it reached the statute book the 1974 Labour government had come into office. It promptly took over the previous government's measure without alteration, and with the Housing Act 1974 the great expansion began.

The movement had already been growing, and Shelter, the National Campaign for the Homeless, had played a notable part in that growth, raising some £3 million by national appeals in 1969 and 1970, which it used mainly to start housing associations in areas of severe housing stress to supplement the provision which the local authorities were making.

By 1971 housing associations were providing an extra 10,000 dwellings a year, a big increase on what they had managed previously. But with the impetus given by the financial arrangements of the 1974 Act, and the work of the Housing Corporation, this figure was more than trebled by 1976, with 35,300 completions. Since then, however, there have been the drastic cuts in public expenditure and some diversion of resources to conversions for sale. New dwelling completions were actually down to 9,700 in 1982-83.

Housing associations have an excellent record in catering for special groups such as the elderly, the handicapped, single persons, and single parent families. They have made a striking contribution to the rehabilitation of older properties in the inner cities. Equally important is their willingness to house families who may be excluded from local authority consideration because they have not lived in an area for the required time; for it has to be admitted that local authorities often have an understandable but possibly excessive preference for 'looking after their own'.

Housing association finance

The 1974 Act introduced an entirely new subsidy system for housing associations. Previous arrangements had been for annual subsidies to meet part of their running costs. This one, tactfully avoiding the pejorative expression 'subsidy', was for a capital 'grant', referred to as HAG (housing association grant). It was of such an amount that the rent, a fair rent fixed by the rent officer, would cover repairs, management, and loan charges on that small fraction of the capital costs which was not met by grant, and therefore needed to be financed by borrowing.

Thus, the main factors are the capital cost of the dwelling, and the rent which will be charged.

Suppose, for example, the dwelling costs £30,000 and that it will command a rent of £25 a week, £1,300 a year. If, say, £500 a year will be needed for repairs and management, £800 will be left available for servicing a loan. That sum will meet loan charges on a loan of about £7,250. So a capital grant of £22,750 – 76 per cent of the capital cost – is needed, and £7,250 will be borrowed. Capital grants are, in fact, usually 75 to 85 per cent of the cost of providing a dwelling (more in London). Since housing associations do not have the same facilities for borrowing as councils, they do not raise loans from individuals and financial institutions as councils do. They may look to the council to advance any balance not met by capital grant and the council may oblige. If it does not, the Housing Corporation will make the necessary loan.

The subsidy arrangements are remarkably generous, and the housing association movement was scarcely able to believe its good fortune. It has to be recognised, however, that the associations need special treatment if they are to provide the required expansion, since they do not have the same large proportion of earlier-built low-cost housing as councils.

Nor do they have a general rate fund on which they can draw if the year's working results in a deficit. So there can be a second subsidy, the revenue deficit subsidy. Despite the favourable capital grant system it is quite possible for an association to find itself with a deficit, especially if it has come into existence only recently, for there will be administrative and other costs before the rent income begins to come in. The association will need to make a case to the Department of the Environment on each year's operations; the grant is not a continuing one, unless it can be shown that the need persists.

How the capital grant works

In practice, since the association will not have sufficient funds of its own, it will need to raise a temporary loan from the Housing Corporation for the purchase of the site (if the scheme is to build new houses), for its own development costs (salaries, fees and so on for the preparation of the scheme), and further amounts to pay the builder as the building work proceeds. There will be interest to pay on the borrowed money, and this too will be 'capitalised', i.e. met by further borrowing.

When the scheme is completed, capital grant (HAG) is applied for, and when this is received it is used to pay off most of the money borrowed. What is left will constitute the long-term loan requirement on the scheme, repayable over 60 years by a combined payment of interest and principal, like the repayments on a building society mortgage. This borrowing will be, as already stated, from the local council or from the Housing Corporation.

The same arrangements apply when the scheme is for acquiring and improving existing dwellings, except that in such cases repayment will be over 30 years, not 60 years.

Grant redemption fund

There was one astonishing oversight in the 1974 Act arrangements. We live in inflationary times, and rents rise significantly at regular intervals. A capital grant which is appropriate when it is given will be too generous for the circumstances a few years later, when rents will have gone up substantially. Yet the subsidy has all been given in one lump sum. The money has gone; it cannot, like an annual subsidy, be reduced for future years when the need is less. Clearly, in times like these the capital grant system is singularly inappropriate.

The light eventually dawned on the DoE, and the Housing Act 1980 requires housing associations in future to keep a grant redemption fund, into which surpluses arising from increased rent income must be paid. The DoE will then, it is hoped, be able to get some of its money back.

Rent levels

The fair rents which housing associations must charge were often higher than those for comparable council dwellings, and the difference could be substantial. It is generally the practice of the associations to make available to the local council a proportion of the vacancies which arise – 50 per cent is quite usual – for applicants on the council's waiting list when the local council has provided loan facilities. So an applicant for a council house may be offered a housing association house. Not surprisingly, such applicants see no good reason why rents should be several pounds a week higher in one case than in the other, for entirely comparable dwellings. They do not see why two landlords in the same area, both supported by the public purse, should have two different levels of rent. Clearly, they should not.

Council tenants with low incomes are helped by housing benefits in the form of rent rebates, reductions in the rents payable. Housing association tenants are treated like the tenants of private landlords; instead of a rent rebate they receive a rent allowance.

This is calculated on exactly same factors as for a rent rebate, but the help takes the form of an actual payment to the tenant, not a reduction in rent payable. The assessment, and the payment, are the responsibility of the local authority. The housing association is not involved, and does not know, or need to know, anything of the tenant's circumstances, or indeed whether he or she is in receipt of a rent allowance or not. For further details, see Chapter 4.

Private rented sector

Background

In 1984 roughly 1.9 million households were living in the private rented sector. The sector was made up broadly as follows:

	No. of households (million)
Unfurnished	1.1
Furnished (both resident and non-resident landlords)	0.35
'Tied' properties provided by employers	0.45
	1.9

We are mainly concerned here with the 1.1 million unfurnished tenancies.

At the outbreak of the first world war renting was the normal tenure, accounting for 90 per cent of the stock, with only 10 per cent owner occupied, few council houses, and a tiny amount of housing association accommodation, provided mainly by charities. By 1983, that 90 per cent had shrunk to 9.1 per cent. It continues to decline steadily, every year without exception, as houses are sold for owner occupation or become unfit, and no new ones are added.

From about 7.1m privately rented homes in 1914, the number fell to 6.6m in 1938, 4.6m in 1960, 1.9m today. Small though it is, the sector is still important, especially in London, but it is shrinking there, as everywhere else.

The House Condition Survey of 1981 found that 63 per cent of the dwellings in this sector had been built before 1919. It contained a far larger proportion of unsatisfactory accommodation than any other sector: 13.5 per cent lacked one or more of the basic amenities, 42 per cent was in substantial disrepair, and just under 18 per cent was unfit for human habitation. Disrepair was a growing problem.

This is a shocking state of affairs, and the reasons – largely financial – make a tangled and discreditable story.

In 1915 rents were frozen, and tenants could not be evicted. The introduction of controlled tenancies was intended as a temporary war-time measure, but tenants were many, landlords few, and government after government refused to face up to the situation produced by the freezing of rents whilst incomes and costs rose. Other countries had had to impose rent control, but none behaved as ineptly as Britain, which neither compensated landlords for lost income nor allowed rents to rise as incomes rose.

Building for rent was already tailing off before 1914: other more attractive fields for investment had appeared. And rent control, in the rigid and inequitable form it took, ensured that no sensible investor would put money into rented housing; and no landlord, when a property became vacant, would think of re-letting if he could sell. If the intention had been to destroy the private rented sector, no more effective strategy could have been devised.

At long intervals small and quite inadequate rent increases had been permitted, but in 1957 the Conservative government decided on a more radical approach. It passed an Act which lifted the controls on properties (de-controlled properties) above a certain rateable value, and on properties below these values when tenants left. It was hoped this would restore the private rented sector by restoring incentives. Capital would flow into rented property; landlords would hold on to an attractive investment instead of trying to get rid of it at any price.

It appears to have been completely overlooked that de-control in conditions of serious scarcity would open the door to widespread exploitation; and a new word, 'Rachmanism', came into the English language as a result of the activities of one of the more unscrupulous and unsavoury operators in this field. Moreover, the sector began to decline faster than ever instead of stabilising, since wherever de-control applied the landlord could get rid of his tenant, whose security of tenure was gone. It was infinitely more attractive to sell with vacant possession than to re-let, for who could guarantee that some future government might not re-impose control?

And this is exactly what happened. A Labour government came to power in 1964, and moved swiftly with a temporary holding measure restoring security of tenure and freezing existing rents. But even before then, the Conservative government which enacted the Rent Act 1957 had become alarmed at what was happening; it had set up the Milner Holland Committee to examine the Greater London housing problem, and it would have had to do something itself if it had been returned to office.

Armed with the report of the Milner Holland Committee which appeared in 1965, the new Labour government lost no time. The minister concerned was Richard Crossman, whose Rent Act 1965 was of major importance. His problem was that he could not simply return to the old controlled rents; they were quite inadequate. Nor could he, in conditions of acute scarcity, let market forces settle rent levels. His solution was fair rents, a novel and entirely artificial concept which nevertheless had considerable attractions. Landlords and tenants should wherever possible agree on a rent. Where they could not, a rent officer appointed by the local authority would set a rent which was fair to both landlord and tenant.

The Act did not define a 'fair' rent, but required the rent officer in performing his act of necromancy to ignore the personal circumstances of the tenant, but have regard to the age, character, locality and state of repair of the dwelling, whilst assuming that there was no scarcity of that particular type of property. Crossman's own rough description of his intention was a rent which would represent a market rent if supply and demand roughly balanced. There was a right of appeal to a rent assessment committee if either party did not agree with the rent officer's assessment.

In the early days most of the applications came from tenants, and the rent officers happily set about reducing rents; but the staffing of the rent assessment committees was carried out by civil servants, and a valuer, Sir Sidney Littlewood, was appointed chairman of the London committee. He set the tone for rent assessment committee valuations, overturning the rents fixed by rent officers in vast numbers, and greatly increasing them. Rent officers got the message. Thereafter it was mainly landlords, not tenants, who came to the rent officer asking him to set fair rents for their properties.

Crossman was not pleased with the way things were turning out, but continued to maintain that his fair rent idea was basically sound. However, the disquiet was sufficient for the Labour government to set up the Francis Committee in 1969, to consider how the Rent Act 1965 was working. It reported in 1971 (by which time the Conservative government was in power), saying that a lot of rent officers were unable to quantify scarcity, and therefore did not discount for it (though this had been an essential element in the Crossman formula). It concluded nevertheless that all was well.

The 1970 Conservative government accepted the Francis Report with alacrity, and its Housing Finance Act 1972, besides providing that the fair rent concept should apply to council housing, also provided that the remainder of the old controlled tenancies which had not yet passed into the regulated tenancy system (regulated tenancies are those for which a fair rent has been registered) should do so over a period, by phasing dependent on rateable value. However this phased transfer was halted when Labour came to power in 1974, and it was the intention to review the working of the Rent Acts before any further changes were made.

But with the election of the 1979 Conservative government and the passing of the Housing Act 1980, the situation changed yet again.

Effects of the Housing Act 1980

Under the 1965 Act, a landlord could only seek registration of a fair rent on a change of tenancy, and the position of existing controlled tenants was preserved. The Housing Act 1969 then increased the scope of the new scheme by enabling landlords to apply for fair rent registration where a dwelling had all the standard amenities and was in a reasonable condition. The Housing Finance Act 1972, as already mentioned, was taking the process further until Labour called a halt.

Now section 64 of the 1980 Act has completed the process. All the remaining 400,000 controlled tenancies were converted at a stroke to regulated tenancies, liable for fair rents, regardless of their condition.

Several other changes were made to the private rented sector by the 1980 Act, the most important of which are:

★ An application for the re-registration of a fair rent can be made after two years instead of three. The permitted rent increase will be half-way to the new rent payable at once, the rest in the following year.

★ A new form of tenancy was introduced, the protected shorthold tenancy, under which landlords could let at fair rents for a fixed term of from one to five years, at the end of which they would have the right to regain possession. After a couple of years, the small number of shorthold tenancies created under the Act led the government to change the rules so that outside London landlords need no longer apply for fair rents; in London, however, the rent registration rule for shorthold tenancies remains in force.

There are thus two kinds of tenancy: the regulated tenancy giving full security of tenure, and the new protected shorthold tenancy where security of tenure ceases at the end of the agreed period. The shorthold system does not apply to existing regulated tenancies.

It is claimed that the effect of allowing shorthold tenancies will be to slow down the decline in the private rented sector by reassuring landlords that it is safe to re-let, knowing that they will be able to regain possession at the end of a relatively short period. However, fair rents are unpopular with many landlords and the condition that shorthold tenancies must be registered for a fair rent is likely to put many of them off. In addition, the next Labour government might repeal the shorthold provisions so that shorthold tenants will become normal regulated tenants with full security of tenure. So the most profitable and safest course for landlords is still to sell with vacant possession whenever a vacancy occurs.

★ Another new form of tenancy is provided for under the 1980 Act, the assured tenancy. This applies only to new dwellings although legislation introduced in 1986 aims to extend it to existing dwellings which have been improved and modernised by the landlord. Such a tenancy is not protected or regulated; the landlord can fix such terms as he thinks fit. The first venture into this field has been by the Abbey National Building Society and though they have been able to keep rents lower than expected, such a tenancy is so much less attractive, financially, than home ownership that it has little future within the present housing finance system.

Rent allowances

Private tenants with low incomes are entitled to help with their rents on exactly the same basis as council or housing association tenants, through housing benefits.

Since it would be quite impractical to operate a rent rebate system, with a rent reduction and a claim by the landlord for grant in respect of lost income, however, the housing benefit takes the form of a rent allowance. The tenant applies to the council, and the council assesses his or her rent-paying capacity and makes a regular payment which enables the tenant to pay the full rent.

The system is described in the chapter on housing benefit.

Where we stand now

The effect of the 1980 Act has been to bring all remaining private tenants (except those whose housing is provided by their employer) into the fair rent system. Inevitably, this meant drastic rent increases for controlled tenants. On the first registration of a fair rent for a previously controlled rent there was, in 1981, a staggering fivefold increase from £72 to £386, on average, in England and Wales. In 1984 it was a sixfold increase from £99 to £600 on average.

Landlords have hastened to avail themselves of the benefit of the 1980 Act; but tenants still have security of tenure; and there is no sign that landlords who already charge fair rents are any less anxious than before to sell with vacant possession rather than let, whenever the opportunity occurs.

All regulated tenancies (except shortholds) give security of tenure. But shorthold tenants – those unfortunates entering the private rented sector who are not offered a regulated tenancy – will have security of tenure only for the term of the tenancy, one to five years. If the shorthold system spreads (though it has shown no early signs of doing so) it will doubtless provide a steady stream of future homeless, as tenancies expire.

But one of the biggest question marks over this sector is the growing problem of disrepair and the lack of basic amenities in so many properties. Higher rents might be expected to result in more spending on maintenance; but there does not seem to be any evidence that this has happened.

Nor has the government given any indication of an intention to improve the landlord's tax position which puts him at an impossible disadvantage as compared with both the owner occupied and the public rented sectors. Yet the problem of growing disrepair will not go away. The experience of other countries which have attempted to face up to this problem, moreover, gives no indication that extra help intended to enable the landlord to improve the condition of his properties will in fact be used for that purpose.

The impossible position of a would-be private landlord

This can be simply illustrated. Suppose a landlord can buy or build something for say £30,000, and suppose (most unlikely) that he or she can finance this on as favourable terms as if they were borrowing from a building society for the purchase of a house they intend to live in, and can raise a loan for the full cost. Outgoings, without allowing for any repayment of the loan, will be:

		£
Loan £30,000		
Interest at 12 per cent		3,600
Repairs and maintenance, say		260
Management, say		150
Outgoings	per annum	£4,010
	per week	£77.12

A rent of £77.12 a week gives no profit at all; he must charge well over that.

But you can *buy* a £30,000 house for just over £57 a week, and put aside £260 a year for maintenance:

Building Society loan, £30,000, 25 years, say 12 per cent

		£	£
Mortgage repayments (first year):			
Interest		3,600	
Principal		210	3,810
Repairs and maintenance (as before)			260
			4,070
Less relief at 29 per cent on £3,600 interest			1,044
Outgoings	per annum		£3,026
	per week		£58.20

37

Who is going to pay well over £80 a week for a house that will never be owned, with the certainty of future rent increases, when less than £60 a week will buy it?

It is clear that without subsidies investors will not be interested in providing dwellings for rent; and it is equally clear that there is no prospect whatsoever of such subsidies for private landlords, whatever the government. Political uncertainty about the future is a further disincentive.

Not impossible for all

But if the present system virtually ensures no additional provision of private rented accommodation, this does not mean that all existing private landlords are incurring losses. Many are doing very nicely. They will have acquired the property a long time ago, at a fraction of today's prices, and if they are doing little or no maintenance whilst collecting fair rents, their original investment will be showing a very handsome return. There is always in the offing, too, the prospect of a very substantial capital gain (even if it is taxable) if the tenant leaves and the property can be sold.

In the cities, in London in particular, many are doing even better, sharing the late Rachman's dedication to the untrammelled working of market forces. They simply ignore the Rent Acts, let the property on licence or by some other device, and charge exorbitant rents, often for very poor accommodation. And the tenant has no security of tenure. The practice of many landlords of splitting a house up into a number of single lets, with tenants having to share facilities, is a further highly profitable variation as is the growing use of 'bed and breakfast' type hostels. With furnished lettings, the overcharging and the insecurity of tenure are even worse. According to a recent Greater London Council survey, half of new private rented sector lettings now fall outside the protection of the Rent Acts.

Housing Benefit

HOUSING IS EXPENSIVE. The average new house these days costs around £35,000 – more than three and a half times average male earnings. Without some form of subsidy or financial help, most people would not be able to afford a decent home.

Acceptance of the need for subsidies for houses built for letting was a matter of consensus from 1919 for the next 60 years, with some six million dwellings built under such arrangements, mostly by councils, some by housing associations. But there was little building for the private rented sector after 1919; rents were controlled; and no government saw any need to subsidise private landlords.

The housing subsidies encouraged councils to build, and enabled them to charge rents which, it was assumed, tenants would be able to pay. These were 'general' subsidies, that is to say, they kept rent levels down for council tenants generally, and took no account of the differing circumstances of individual tenants.

Needs related allowances for housing costs begin

In 1966 the government introduced a scheme to help low-income domestic ratepayers, for many of whom the rates had become a serious burden. It took the form of rate rebates (reductions in the amount payable), according to the income and family circumstances of the ratepayer. Government grant met 90 per cent of the cost; local authorities provided the balance.

Meanwhile, in spite of housing subsidies the rent levels of many councils were imposing hardship on numbers of poorer tenants (private tenants were still sheltered by rent controls) and some of the more perceptive councils had been introducing their own methods of assistance. These were rent rebate schemes of various kinds, taking account of ability to pay and giving rent reductions, rather like the rate rebate system. There was no government subsidy for these local schemes, so the cost was met either by rate contributions, or by the remaining tenants.

In 1972 the Conservative government changed the housing subsidy system and at the same time required council rents to rise to the 'fair rent' levels which by now applied to much of the private rented sector. Since many tenants already needed help, it was obvious that more help would be needed as rents rose, so a national rent rebate scheme was provided for, applying to all councils. The cost was largely met by government grant, at first 75 per cent, later 90 per cent.

But private sector rents were also rising sharply, as 'fair rents' replaced the old 'controlled' rents, so help was needed there, too. The private landlord could not be expected to operate a means test, give rent reductions, and then claim on the government for lost income. The solution, therefore, was rent allowances, actual payments to low-income tenants to enable them to pay the full rent, based on exactly the same factors used in calculating rebates. Councils were given the job of administering the new system, as well as their own rent rebates. The full cost of these rent allowances was met by the government.

There was still, however, a large group of tenants who were not covered by rent rebates or allowances. These were people in receipt of supplementary benefits from the DHSS. Their benefits had been set at levels which were deemed sufficient to allow them to pay their inclusive rents (the rent plus rates) in full, and this continued unchanged.

There was yet another class of householder outside the rent rebate or allowance system – the low-income mortgagor. He or she could be entitled to a rate rebate, and if supplementary benefits were payable the interest part of the mortgage repayments (but not the principal) could be included in the supplementary benefit figure.

To recapitulate, in this jungle of complication which had grown up:
★ council tenants could receive rebates (i.e. reduction) in rent and rates;

★ private tenants could receive allowances (actual payments from the council) to enable them to pay the rent and rates in full;

★ tenants receiving supplementary benefits, whether public or private, did not receive rebates or allowances; they paid in full, with their benefits pitched at levels which allowed them to do so;

★ owner-occupiers, whether with a mortgage or owning outright, could be entitled to rate rebates; and those with a mortgage could also be helped with the interest part of the mortgage repayments if they were on supplementary benefits.

The arrival of housing benefits

There were two public bodies administering these schemes – local councils, and the DHSS. The assessment of entitlement to rent rebates and rent allowances was different from that used to determine supplementary benefit payments. One system could give more help than the other, but few tenants were in a position to know which suited them best. In 1979 it was estimated that 400,000 households were worse off because they were receiving the wrong benefit. The government proposal in 1981 to replace the dual system by a 'unified housing benefit' scheme, to be administered by councils alone, therefore, was widely welcomed.

Unfortunately the scheme got off to a bad start. It was obvious that it would cost money to put right the existing anomalies, yet the Treasury insisted that the new scheme must cost no more than the old ones. Anomalies could, they claimed, be put right by changes within the overall scheme. This was attempted – making the poor responsible for helping the very poor – but the changes created new anomalies, the new system became more and more complicated, and it was soon clear that its implications had not been worked out in detail. Nor was enough time allowed for the enormous task of setting up the new scheme with the result that its introduction was an administrative disaster, causing great hardship to hundreds of thousands of claimants. Press comments were scathing, and even the government's own backbenchers described the affair as 'an act of gross social and political folly'.

As if to add insult to injury, the government immediately started to seek cuts in benefit levels for the new scheme. Following an outcry about both the government's proposals and priorities, ministers announced a review of the housing benefit scheme – less than a year after it had come fully into force. This review subsequently became part of the government's general review of the social security system, and major changes to the housing benefit scheme have been proposed. These are looked at in more detail later.

How the housing benefit scheme works

'Housing benefit' is the collective name for the several means of helping low-income householders with their housing costs.

Each local council is now responsible for all arrangements to assist tenants (the overwhelming majority of cases), and for rate rebates for owner-occupiers. The two largest groups of benefit claimants are standard cases, which are all those not in receipt of supplementary benefits, and certificated cases, which are those who do claim supplementary benefits, for whom the DHSS issues certificates to the council (hence the name).

To illustrate how the scheme works, we start with a *standard case* claiming help with the rent. A claim form has to be filled in by the applicant giving details of income and particulars of those living in the house.

First, the applicant's *gross income* must be stated. This is the weekly earnings, pensions, child benefit, and any other income before deductions. If the applicant is working, a fixed amount is disregarded, ostensibly to allow for items like national insurance and other work expenses which, of course, reduce the gross wage to the amount the wage earner actually takes home. The gross income, less any 'disregards', is the 'adjusted income'.

Next, the adjusted income is compared with the applicant's *needs allowance*, based on national scales which allow for size of family, and any special factors such as the age or disability of a member of the household.

If the applicant's adjusted income is equal to the needs allowance, the applicant is deemed to be able to pay 40 per cent of the rent, and will be entitled to a rebate of the other 60 per cent.

If the adjusted income is below the needs allowance, the rebate will be increased by so many pence (according to a standard formula) for every pound the income falls below the needs allowance.

If, however, the income is above the needs allowance, the rebate will be reduced by so many pence (again according to a standard formula) for each pound above the needs allowance. It will also be reduced if there is someone living in the house who is not dependent on the applicant (for example grown-up children with jobs of their own), since non-dependants are assumed to be making a contribution to the rent.

In the case of a couple with two children, one under 18, one over, husband working and earning £85 a week, wife not working, rent £14 a week, the calculation is as follows. (The benefit rates are those in operation in spring 1986; rates are constantly being changed.)

Gross income	earnings	85.00
	child benefit	7.00
		92.00
	less earnings disregard	17.30
Adjusted income		£74.70
Needs allowance	couple	70.20
	one child	14.50
		£84.70

Adjusted income is £10 less than the applicant's needs allowance

Benefit entitlement:	
basic amount 60 per cent of £14 rent	8.40
add 25p for each pound income falling below needs allowance	2.50
	10.90
less reduction for non-dependent (the child over 18)	7.80
	£3.10

So this council tenant will be expected to pay a rent of £10.90 a week, (£14 less rent rebate of £3.10).

There is a similar calculation for the rate rebate, with 40 per cent again being the amount for which a ratepayer will be liable if the adjusted income is equal to the needs allowance.

But whereas a rent rebate increases by 25p for every pound that income falls short of the needs allowance, the rate rebate increases by only 8p.

Similarly where income is more than the needs allowance, a rent rebate is reduced by 29p for every pound of the excess, but the rate rebate is reduced by only 13p. So for every pound in excess of the needs allowance, the tenant's help is reduced in total by 42p.

We have assumed that the applicant is a council tenant. For private landlord or housing association applicants the calculations are exactly the same, but instead of a reduction in the rent and rates the benefit takes the form of a payment of £3.10 a week by the council to the tenant, so that the tenant can pay in full.

Certificated cases

Anyone who is receiving supplementary benefit is entitled to have their main housing costs met in full through housing benefit. For tenants this will be their rent and rates; for home-owners, whether owning outright or still with a mortgage, the benefit covers their rate payments only. Home owners with a mortgage – though not entitled to housing benefit from the council towards their mortgage repayments – will, if they are on supplementary benefit, receive an extra amount in the supplementary benefit they receive from the DHSS to cover the interest on the mortgage. All home owners on supplementary benefit also get small sums to help with house insurance and repairs, and these payments too will come from the DHSS.

When someone is claiming supplementary benefit, the council is notified by the DHSS by means of a certificate, and the council meets the claimant's rent and rates in full. For council tenants this means that they will receive a notice from the council telling them what the rent and rates are, but that they are not expected to make a payment. Private landlord and housing association tenants receive a payment from the council equivalent to the inclusive rent (rent and rates combined), so that they can pay the landlord in full. Home owners who are certificated cases will receive details of their rate demand, and an indication that no payment is to be made.

Local councils are reimbursed in full by government grant for the payment of housing benefits to certificated cases, plus 0.6 per cent to cover the administrative cost of the work, which they have taken over from the DHSS.

Housing benefit supplement

Although the housing benefit scheme was supposed to unify the previous systems of rebates, allowances, and supplementary benefit payments, all it actually unified was their administration – which has become solely the responsibility of the local authority – while the structure of the scheme has stayed pretty much the same. Some people who are now only entitled to claim housing benefit would have been better off if they were, as previously, entitled to claim supplementary benefits. To deal with this situation an additional payment, housing benefit supplement, was introduced. It is administered and paid by the council, but as it is a supplementary benefit payment it is assessed by the DHSS. It is very important to those entitled to it, since besides providing extra money it also entitles the recipient to a range of other benefits, including help with NHS charges and free school meals for the children. The system is complicated and confusing to both the public and those who administer it, and since applicants are often unaware of their entitlement, it is vital that housing benefit staff should be able to identify them and refer them to the DHSS.

Other charges

Housing benefits are also paid towards some other housing costs in certain circumstances, including water rates and heating charges. For more information the many guides available at post offices and DHSS offices should be consulted.

Government plans for changes

Major changes to the housing benefit scheme are being planned by the government as part of its restructuring of the social security system. At the time of writing the government's Social Security Act has just received royal assent, and the following changes will be implemented by 1988. There have already been many cuts in benefits, some of them, in the opinion of many informed commentators, harsh beyond any rational explanation other than the alleged pressing need to cut public expenditure.

Unification of the scheme

The two main groups in the present housing benefit scheme – certificated cases and standard cases – will be unified so that they are assessed in the same way. Assessments of benefit will be based on net income – after tax and national insurance contributions have been deducted – rather than gross income as at present. (Incidentally, it is a glaring anomaly in the present arrangements that tax can be levied on wages so low that the wage earner needs benefits to bring those wages up to a minimum living standard.) Net income will be compared to the supplementary benefit rate to which the family would be entitled.

If income is equal to supplementary benefit entitlement, rent and rates will be paid at the maximum level of assistance (see next section). For every pound that the applicant's net income is above supplementary benefit level, a proportion of rebate (or allowance) will be withdrawn; although final details are not yet known the government has suggested withdrawing benefit at the rate of 60p for every pound for rent, and 20p for every pound for rates.

Maximum level of assistance

At the moment, people on supplementary benefit have their rent and rates met in full. The government is proposing that this should continue for rent payments, but for rates the maximum level of assistance should be set at 80 per cent, so that everyone will pay at least 20 per cent of their rates bill.

Subsidies to local authorities

The government originally proposed to reduce the level of subsidy paid to local authorities to 80 per cent of costs. At the time of writing, this proposal has been withdrawn but no new plans put in its place. At present the subsidy is 100.6 per cent of certificated housing benefit payments, and 90 per cent of standard benefit payments. Since the whole cost of support for incomes should be borne by national taxation rather than local rates, the rationale of this proposal is not immediately apparent. What is clear, however, is that any cuts of this sort will penalise already deprived areas much more than prosperous ones.

Changes to supplementary benefit

In addition to the above changes in the housing benefit scheme, the government is also proposing to reduce the help given with housing costs through the supplementary benefit system. Help with 'residual' housing costs for home owners is to be ended, and the government is seeking ways to reduce the level of support given to low-income home owners through payment of the interest element in mortgage repayments; but it is not proposing to alter the lavish subsidy to high-income mortgagors (of up to 60 per cent of the mortgage interest) given by tax relief.

Changes to supplementary benefit rates of payment – which will be the new 'needs allowance' for housing benefit calculations – are also proposed, and will affect entitlement to rebates or allowances under the new unified scheme. Cuts in supplementary benefit levels for young single people under 25, for example, will also mean cuts in entitlement for help with housing costs.

Owner occupied sector

OWNER OCCUPATION is now by far the largest sector, accounting for 13.2 million dwellings, just over 60 per cent of the housing stock. It is also the most popular, and this is not surprising, for not only does it offer the householder more choice and freedom than any other tenure, but it is also the most profitable investment that any ordinary person ever makes. The make-up of this sector at the end of 1984 was broadly as follows.

	millions	%
Owned with a building society mortgage	6.3	48
Owned with some other mortgage	1.3	10
Owned outright	5.5	42
	13.2	100

Because the growth in owner-occupation has been linked so closely with the growth of the building society movement, and because the great majority of houses are purchased with a building society loan, we begin here with a description of how the societies operate.

Growth of the building societies

All houses are bought on borrowed money, usually with a loan from a building society, less frequently from a local authority, a bank, or an insurance company.

Building societies started in a small way in the 19th century and made little progress until after the first world war, when their expansion really started. But this was as nothing to what followed the second world war, and even more so during the explosive growth of the last 20 years.

Building societies – total assets

	£ million
1900	60
1920	87
1940	756
1960	3,166
1980	53,793
1984	102,689

Source: Building Societies Association Bulletin No. 45, January 1986

In earlier years there were some colourful characters in the industry – not a bit like it is today – and there were some spectacular (and sometimes hilarious) episodes involving fraud. But the dramatic success of the last 20 odd years has been solidly built on a first rate service to savers, a reputation for sound management and complete reliability, and highly attractive investment terms. The privileged tax position (see later) has helped, too. There has also been for some years a very sensible arrangement whereby the societies act together to ensure that no investor is involved in a loss in those rare cases when a society gets into difficulties; and consequently the movement deservedly enjoys the full confidence of investors.

The way building societies work

At first sight, the whole basis on which building societies operate (accepting money which is mostly repayable on demand or at very short notice, and lending it for long periods) is the opposite of what is normally regarded as sound practice. They are borrowing short to lend long. But there is a safeguard which transforms the situation. Every advance is secured by a mortgage containing a variable interest clause, under which the society can give notice to the borrower at any time of a change in the rate of interest which is charged on the loan. So when interest rates rise, a society can avoid withdrawals by investors who would be attracted by higher rates elsewhere by promptly increasing its own rates. It can afford to do this by giving notice to all its borrowers that the interest they will pay will also go up. The Building Societies Association (BSA), to which virtually all the societies belong, advises what interest rates should be, and the members by and large follow the advice very closely.

Special tax arrangements

One feature, peculiar to building societies until April 1985, was that the interest paid to investors is tax paid. This means that it is treated by the Inland Revenue as if tax had already been deducted from it at standard rate before it is paid out. Recipients of such interest, then, are not taxed on it unless they are liable for tax above the standard rate. So seven per cent on 'ordinary shares' is as good as ten per cent on any other investment, on which tax would have to be paid.

This does not mean that building societies are lending at 12.75 per cent, using money which has cost them only seven per cent. They have to account to the Inland Revenue for the tax which is deemed to have been deducted. But they only hand over part of it. If they had to account for it at the standard rate of 29 per cent (as, for instance, local authorities have to on the interest they pay on their loans) then that seven per cent, worth ten per cent gross to the investor, would be costing the building societies ten per cent. But it does not. Since 1894, building societies have a unique and (for them) happy arrangement for paying less tax than anyone else – although since April 1985 they have had to share this advantage with the banks.

Income tax in those far-off days was 4d (less than 2p) in the pound, and the Inland Revenue wanted to know how much interest was being paid, and to whom, so that they could tax it. The building societies were deeply shocked. To give this confidential information would, they protested, 'be disastrous to the business of the building societies and lead to considerable withdrawals of investments therein', and they steadfastly refused to co-operate, and went on refusing for years.

However, as everyone knows, there is no limit to the ruthlessness of the avaricious tax gatherers, and these unscrupulous people came along in 1894 with a proposal to tax the profits of building societies. This so alarmed the societies that they made a voluntary agreement to account for tax at half rate on the interest they paid out. This was a rough and ready method of recognising that some investors would be taxable, some not. The Inland Revenue would get its money, or most of it, and save itself a lot of clerical work. The terms varied occasionally, and the whole arrangement had no legal standing until 1952, when it was given statutory authority.

Nowadays the Inland Revenue does a little checking from time to time, and on the basis of this it negotiates with the Building Societies Assocation a rate at which tax will be handed over. This rate is called the composite rate, in recognition of the fact that some investors are not taxable, some are. It is at present 25.25 per cent, as against the standard rate of tax of 29 per cent.

The Inland Revenue is happy, since it is collecting with little trouble about the same total as if some investors were taxed at standard rate, and those on low incomes not at all. The building societies are more than happy; they are getting a concealed subsidy worth 0.5 per cent on their borrowing. But it is really an indefensible arrangement, for that subsidy actually comes from the poorer investors, who receive their interest tax paid, but are not allowed to reclaim tax from the Tax Inspector as they would have been able to do under normal arrangements.

In the last few years the banks have made vigorous inroads into the mortgage market, but unlike the societies they paid interest to their investors without deduction of tax. It was the investors who had to account for tax to the Inland Revenue – unless of course they were not taxable because of low income. But since April 1985 the banks have been put on the same footing as building societies; they have to pay interest net of tax, and account to the Inland Revenue for that tax at the composite rate. So they, too, should make a profit on the new deal.

The borrower and the building society

Would-be home owners, having found a suitable house, will normally approach a building society for a loan. Their reception will be more friendly if they have been investors for some years; if not, they may have to shop around. They used to find that a society would be prepared to lend 75 per cent, perhaps as much as 80 per cent, of the value of the property. Borrowers would have to find the rest themselves, no inconsiderable sum at today's prices. But recently this problem has eased, with many societies prepared to lend 90 per cent or more of the house price. Borrowers will also have to meet some other costs, of course, such as the society's charges for the valuation and preparing the mortgage, and the solicitor's fees for conveyancing.

The building society will wish to assure itself that the borrower is creditworthy, in other words capable of meeting the cost of the repayments. For many years a common measure was that the loan could be 2¼-2½ times the borrower's annual income; so that earnings of £8,000 a year were good for a loan of £18,000-£20,000. If the householder's spouse is working the society will usually be prepared to allow the second income or part of it to be taken into account as well. In 1985 the average advance to first time buyers was £20,260, average dwelling price was £23,742, and average income was £10,466.

It is a very different picture for those who are not first time buyers, but are changing houses. They borrowed on average about £23,300, but the average dwelling price was £39,390, and average income £12,702. They will be older than first time buyers, and presumably on higher wages or salaries; but more important, they will have had a house to sell which will have yielded a handsome capital profit, enabling them to put down a very large amount, over £16,000 on average, towards the cost of a new dwelling.

A building society's security for its advance is a mortgage, a legal document requiring the borrower to make repayments on the terms agreed, with a variable interest clause giving the society the right to vary the rate of interest after due notice. The society also has the right to foreclose (that is, to take possession and sell the property to discharge the outstanding debt) if the borrowers fail to keep their side of the bargain.

Repayment of most mortgages is by what is called the annuity method, an equalised repayment over the life of the loan of interest and principal. Interest is on the amount of outstanding loan. At first, interest is the main element, with principal quite a small item; but as part of the principal is paid off each year, the interest share is a little less and the principal repayment a little more. The whole calculation ensures that by the end of the agreed period, the loan will have been paid off.

In recent years, however, an increasing number of new loans have been on endowment mortgages. Here the borrower pays interest on the original sum borrowed throughout the life of the mortgage, while simultaneously making payments for an insurance policy which, at the end of the mortgage term, yields a lump sum to pay off the mortgage. Until

1983, endowment mortgages were taken out by only a minority of borrowers – around 20 per cent in 1981. But changes in tax relief in April 1983 gave endowments a financial boost, and nearly 60 per cent of new borrowers in 1985 were taking out endowment mortgages. Marketing has also been helped by the development of 'low cost' endowment policies. Endowment mortgages are often portrayed as providing not simply a way of paying off the mortgage – lump sum bonuses are also promised as possibilities. Crucially, though, the insurance policies need to perform 'well' to provide the money needed to meet the mortgage (and the bonus). In fact, many low cost endowments have no guarantee that, at the end of the mortgage term, enough money will be available to pay off the debt.

Local authority mortgages

Councils have had the power to lend money for house purchase since 1899. It was not until after 1945, however, that central government modernised the old unsatisfactory arrangements, and councils began to operate on a similar basis to the well-tried building society practice. They became very successful in this, the volume of business expanded rapidly, and because councils were ready to lend on older property often not acceptable to the building societies, and also to make advances up to 100 per cent of the house price, they were giving a valuable service, especially to borrowers in less favourable financial situations.

However, this service is now negligible as a result of restrictions on local government borrowing. The Treasury, by some unexplained process of reasoning, sees a difference between a council raising money from the public and using it to finance house purchase, and a building society doing precisely the same thing. The former is public sector expenditure, and therefore a bad thing; the latter is not public sector expenditure, and therefore a good thing.

The Housing Act 1980 and council lending

The right to buy and the right to a mortgage which the 1980 Act gives to council tenants have already been referred to in Chapter 1. The Act also prescribes the method by which the interest rate on such mortgages will in future be fixed, a further encroachment on local authority discretion.

The new arrangement applies also to council lending for the purchase of privately owned houses. Councils finance these advances from their loans fund, described in Chapter 1, and in the past the interest they charged to borrowers was normally a little above their loans fund average rate, to allow for administration costs.

For some time, though, councils had wanted freedom to keep more in line with building society rates, even if this meant deficits in some years and surpluses in others, and the Labour government's green paper on housing policy (1977) proposed that they should have this freedom.

The 1980 Act, however, provides for something quite different. The secretary of state will prescribe a 'standard national rate', which is the Building Societies Association recommended rate. The council will have to charge either this rate, or 0.25 per cent above its own loans fund average rate of interest, whichever is the higher.

This is a very odd way of dealing with the business, and one very much to the disadvantage of those mortgagors unfortunate enough to have a council mortgage. If, as has been the position recently, councils do not need, or wish, to charge as high a rate as the societies, they will still have to do so even if this means a considerable profit at the borrower's expense. If the council's own loans fund rate, plus 0.25 per cent, is higher than the building societies are charging, it will have to charge that higher rate. So borrowers will either be paying as much as a building society would charge, though there is no need for it, or they will be paying more. For those who thought of this illogical arrangement it has two attractions – encouraging borrowers to seek building society mortgages and making councils look less effective than the societies.

Owner-occupiers are subsidised

An astonishing number of people still refuse to believe that owner occupiers get any help whatsoever from the public purse. These people can frequently be heard complaining about 'subsidised council tenants', and they take great offence if it is suggested that, as owner occupiers, they are subsidised too. The main subsidy is in the form of mortgage tax relief. This is tax relief (a reduction in a person's tax bill) on mortgage interest, and for those paying the standard rate of tax it is equivalent to a 29 per cent reduction in mortgage interest payments. In the early years of a mortgage, practically all payments are for interest on the loan, rather than repayments of the principal. This tax relief costs the country money in tax income foregone, just as surely as the exchequer subsidies to council houses costs money when they are paid out. The following section explains how this mortgage tax relief subsidy came about.

Schedule A tax and mortgage tax relief

Owner occupiers do not pay rent. Of two people in identical houses worth a rent of £1,000 a year, the person who owns will have £1,000 more to spend than the one who is a tenant.

However, it is sometimes argued that the owner occupier has sacrificed income by putting money into a house instead of investing it in some other way. That is perfectly true. But the owner would have had to pay tax on any investment income received, while no tax is payable on the no less real increase in disposable income which results from owning the house he or she lives in.

It was not always so. The ownership of property always used to be taxed on the rental value (it was called Schedule A tax, as distinct from Schedule E tax which is levied on earnings, or Schedule D tax on profits).

In doing this the Inland Revenue took the easy way out by using rating values as the measure of letting value. This would have been a logical saving of unnecessary duplication if rating values had been kept up-to-date, but they never were. They still do. In the post-war years annual ~~unpopularity of revaluation. They still do. In the poast-war years annual~~ rental values for rating and income tax purposes had become a mere fraction of the real rental values, and although income tax continued to be levied on a theoretical rental value, the amounts were much less than they should have been. In 1955 a Royal Commission on the Taxation of Profits and Income considered the problem and recommended that the tax on the benefit of ownership (on what they called the 'imputed rental') was right, and should continue as an element in a fair taxation system.

Nevertheless in 1963 parliament chose to ignore this, and abolished Schedule A income tax. It was not thought right to tax a person on a rent which was not actually collected; and anyway the tax was not providing much revenue. (And no wonder.) Since then, ownership has conferred a tax-free addition to the income of a householder who owns outright.

However, a householder might not own outright, but be in the process of buying, usually with the help of a loan from a building society. Such a person was the owner in a legal sense, but in practical terms was only a part owner, still in the process of acquiring the house. It would clearly not have been equitable to tax mortgagors as if they owned outright, because although they saved themselves a rent they had to meet repayments on their mortgages. They were not yet receiving the full benefits of ownership.

The solution had presented no difficulty. In accordance with normal taxation practice mortgagors were being taxed under Schedule A but were entitled to a reduction of the assessment in respect of the interest being paid on the mortgages. In other words, they were entitled to tax relief on mortgage interest.

When Schedule A tax was abolished, there remained no logical reason for mortgage tax relief. But parliament is nothing if not resilient, and this little local difficulty scarcely gave them pause. Relief was justified, it was said, because mortgage interest is paid out of taxed income. But no one suggested that rents, which are also paid out of taxed income, should attract tax relief.

A second argument was advanced. Owner occupation is a good thing in itself, and should be encouraged. This second argument concedes in effect that tax relief on mortgage interest is a subsidy, but is justified because home ownership deserves subsidising. All parties agreed, and liability to tax under Schedule A disappeared; but tax relief on mortgage interest remained, though the fiscal justification for it had gone.

The susceptibilities of the mortgagor were, however, borne in mind. Instead of the cost of tax relief on mortgage interest being shown in the housing chapter of the Public Expenditure White Paper as a cost to the Exchequer, it is tactfully ignored. A reduction of tax revenues is not public expenditure, though it obviously has the same effect.

There is nothing wrong with the principle of assisting home ownership. What has been wrong, and dishonest, is the constant stressing of the heavy cost of subsidies to council tenants, as if these subsidies increased the burden on the general taxpayer whilst tax concessions to mortgagors did not; and this at a time when the two tenures were subsidised about equally. Since then the changes made by the Housing Act 1980 have altered things drastically. The enormous rent increases and subsidy reductions for council tenants, without a corresponding halt to the rising cost of tax relief, means that the average mortgagor now gets several times as much help as the average council tenant. And the gap widens every year.

How tax relief is given

There are some owner-occupiers, mainly in old terraced properties, whose incomes are so low that they are not liable for income tax. Until 1968 the preposterous position was that since they paid no tax they could not be entitled to tax relief. They alone, the poorest, were the only mortgagors so that their costs were no higher than they would have been if they had received tax relief at the standard rate.

~~enabled the building society to reduce interest charges to low income mortgageors so that their costs were no higher than they would have been if they had received tax relief at the standard rate.~~

The end result was roughly the same for both classes of mortgagor. But whereas the option mortgage cases paid interest at a reduced rate to the building society (which got subsidy to make up the difference), the rest paid the building society in full. Their help came by a reduction in their tax bill. Moreover, those on higher incomes who paid tax at a higher rate received help at the highest rate they paid – most help for those with the highest incomes, a decidedly odd way of subsidising housing.

From April 1983 the system was changed by the introduction of MIRAS (mortgage interest relief at source). All mortgagors now pay reduced interest to the building society as if they were option mortgage cases, and the building society is reimbursed for the lost income by the Exchequer. The reduction assumes tax at 29 per cent, and mortgagors no longer need a reduction in their tax bill, unless, of course, they were previously receiving help at more than 29 per cent because their highest rate of tax was more than that. Higher rate taxpayers now get some help through reduced interest charges, like other borrowers, and further help by a reduction in their tax bills. The existing anomaly, most help for those with the highest incomes, was carefully preserved.

Other tax privileges for owner occupiers

Besides mortgage interest tax relief, home ownership is also favourably treated by its exemption from liability to Capital Gains Tax. This is normally payable on any asset sold at a profit – stocks and shares for instance. But it does not apply to the sale of a house in which the vendor lived. This relief was estimated by the Treasury to be worth £2,500 millions in 1985/86.

Owning a home as an investment

Ownership is the perfect hedge against inflation, for the house buyer's costs are mainly mortgage repayments, and these depend on the amount borrowed when the house was first bought. Mortgage repayments continue to be made on the amount that was borrowed then. Of course interest rates change, up to a record 15 per cent not long ago, but now down to 11 per cent. Rents never come down. Furthermore, as the years go by the interest element in the mortgage repayments decreases as the principal element increases, and the borrower is less affected by interest rate changes than in the early years.

Take the case of a person who bought in 1970. The average price of all dwellings, new and existing, was around £5,000, and a loan would probably have been raised on such a house at 8.5 per cent interest. Mortgage repayments on £4,000 would be £392 a year at first, less mortgage tax relief. Interest rates fluctuated over the years, but the repayments would, thanks to tax relief, have always been less than £500 a year, £10 a week. The rent of an average council house is over £14 at the time of writing and will be more the year after, and go on increasing for ever for a house which the tenant will never own. But mortgage repayments will cease altogether at the end of the mortgage period.

And this is not all. A house which was worth £5,000 in 1970 will on average be worth £35,000 in 1985 – a sevenfold increase. While the purchaser has been paying out less than £500 a year, £10 a week, for the last 15 years, the house has put on £30,000 in value, an average of £2,000 a year, four times as much as the mortgage repayments. No wonder house purchase is popular.

Another dramatic illustration is the place which home ownership occupies in the personal sector of the national economy. In 1962 it accounted for about 27 per cent of net wealth. By 1984 the figure was 45.7 per cent.

In 1985, house prices rose on average by 10 per cent, twice the rate of inflation. In early 1986 the building societies, instead of having to raise money solely through the savings of individuals, were allowed to borrow from financial institutions, a new freedom which they exercised with some vigour. Mortgage queues vanished; the societies, the banks, and new forms of lenders began to compete against one another in an unprecedented way. This may not turn out to be an unmixed blessing, for it seems certain to give a further sharp impetus to the upward spiral of house prices. Those already well housed will be highly gratified. Would-be first-time buyers, with little chance of renting as an alternative, will be in greater difficulties than they were before.

Overview

Housing is different

IN CONSIDERING the present financial arrangements for housing, it is necessary first to remember its special characteristics.

Housing is what economists call a durable commodity, unlike for example food and drink, or semi-durable commodities like motor cars or washing machines. Its length of life – for practical purposes only land has a longer life – makes it unique. This is particularly important when the rate of inflation is very high. One consequence of this, in the case of durable commodities like houses, is that instead of them becoming worth less as they grow older (and nearer the time they will have to be replaced), their value in money terms gets steadily greater.

Over the last 20 years, house prices have risen dramatically. The householder who bought in 1970 paid on average about £5,000. By 1975 the house was worth on average £12,000, by 1980 £24,300, and by 1985 £33,800.

There are other factors besides inflation, of course, which affect prices. A shortage of building society funds will slow down price increases; and an excess of funds is widely regarded as being behind the fantastic increases of 1972 and 1973.

The steady pressure of demand for such a socially and financially attractive investment also increases prices. In theory, where there is an excess of demand the effect of market forces is to increase the supply; and as this happens, prices should fall, or at least cease to increase so rapidly. Unfortunately for theory, housing demonstrates another singular and unhelpful characteristic – the supply cannot be increased rapidly; it is 'inelastic'. However great the scarcity, whatever the demand, the size of the housing stock grows by not more than two per cent a year. At present, thanks to the unprecedented restrictions imposed by government on council building, the increase is rather less than one per cent.

There have been other factors too which from time to time have had an effect on the housing market. There was the need for rapid provision of cheap housing for the labour force required by the industrial revolution; and, following this, the realisation by our Victorian forebears that smallpox, typhoid and cholera germs did not, regrettably, distinguish between persons of different social classes, so that minimum standards of sanitation and space had to be imposed for urban settlements. And finally in this century there has been a growing awareness, translated into action, that decent housing is necessary for a civilised society, and essential for an efficient industrial economy.

Housing cannot safely be left to market forces. Of course, the market does work in the case of houses for sale; but that market is affected by the tax privileges which an owner-occupier enjoys and the ready availability of mortgage finance from a highly developed building society industry, and more recently from the banks.

All this produces disproportionate increases in house prices, to the great satisfaction of those who have already bought, whilst creating serious obstacles for many of those who are trying to gain entry into the tenure.

Thanks to rent controls the market is not allowed to work at all in part of the private rented sector; but where landlords evade the restrictions of the Rent Act, as a growing number of them are doing, the market does work. And a very unattractive spectacle it is, with gross exploitation of scarcity at the expense of the poorest.

In the case of councils and housing associations, social considerations have been paramount, at least up to 1980, and the market has been seen as irrelevant. Since then the picture has been changing rapidly, as direct government intervention has forced rents upwards.

Loan debt

The building of council houses and the building or buying of privately owned ones is financed by borrowing. There is a difference, however. Council houses stay in one ownership; privately owned houses change hands on average every seven or eight years, always for a higher price than before.

This means that the loan debt which finances the original cost of a council house (the 'historic' cost) does not increase, indeed it will eventually be paid off. And throughout the life of the loan, the loan charges will always be based on that original loan debt. On earlier built low-cost houses the loan charges will be very small; on later, more expensive ones, very large. Overall, the average loan debt for each of England's five million council dwellings is only £5,750. (The houses themselves, according to DoE estimates in 1984 were worth on average £20,800.)

With privately owned houses the situation is completely different. Values are rising all the time, and ownership is changing frequently, so the loan debt constantly increases. An ever growing volume of savings is needed to finance it, and this results in a steadily increasing cost in tax relief. There is a constant 'gearing up' as values rise and ownership changes take place. Building society figures show the change.

	Number of advances outstanding	Mortgage debt outstanding	
		In total	Average per borrower
1974	4,250,000	£16,030m	£3,771
1984	6,317,000	£81,879m	£12,692

The number of borrowers has gone up by 48.6 per cent, but total mortgage debt is up by 410.8 per cent.

Help to the main sectors

For the private rented sector, there are neither subsidies nor tax relief.

For council housing, there have been annual subsidies from the exchequer, the purpose of which was to enable councils to charge 'reasonable' rents within the rent-paying capacity of the average tenant. Many councils, but by no means all, have also provided contributions from the rates. This was often no more than is justified in meeting costs charged to the Housing Revenue Account which in equity should be borne by the community at large, not just the tenants; but some councils also gave rate aid to keep rent levels down to what they considered to be reasonable levels.

The way the Housing Act 1980 has been implemented has altered the picture completely. Rent increases have been so great that outside London subsidies from the exchequer are virtually no longer payable; and by the same token, far from rate aid being required, most HRAs are now in surplus.

Housing associations get once-for-all subsidies, referred to as 'capital grants', which meet most of the cost of building. Some of them also receive annual revenue deficit subsidy.

For home-buyers, tax relief on their mortgage interest is a subsidy which now imposes a very heavy burden on the exchequer – some £4,750 millions in 1985-86 and growing by hundreds of millions each year.

In 1976 exchequer subsidies averaged £174 per mortgagor and £135 per council tenant. But by 1985-86 house-purchasers, with incomes twice as high on average as those of council tenants; with the considerable advantage of an investment which grows rapidly in value as the real cost of mortgage repayments declines; with outgoings which cease at the end of the mortgage period; were getting around five times as much help from the public purse as council tenants.

Visible and invisible subsidies

An American writer, W C Baer, refers to 'the comparison between the highly visible, contentious, grudgingly given, inflexible and cumbersome 'housing subsidies' to renters, and the unstigmatised, backdoor, low-profile, popular and highly effective tax benefits to home buyers'.

He was talking about America. It's a small world.

In Britain the cost of subsidies to council housing has been a constant topic of chancellors and government ministers. They are also in the habit of referring to the entire housing programme as if it was money provided by the Treasury, whereas nearly half of it is actually capital raised by local authorities themselves, and of course repaid by them over a period.

The cost of subsidising home ownership, on the other hand, is never mentioned. Yet the burden on the exchequer, by decreasing the tax yield, means that the chancellor must raise additional taxes elsewhere to make good the revenue he loses by giving tax relief on mortgage interest. But no chancellor has drawn attention to this in a budget speech even when, as now, the cost is rising so dramatically.

The effects of inflation

The main element in public sector housing costs – loan charges – is not increased by inflation. On the contrary, the real cost of loan charges is falling, and it is this which has enabled councils to let recently built houses (which cost much more than earlier ones) at rents which are in line with those of the rest of the housing stock, and with the rents (at least until the Housing Act 1980 began to operate) keeping roughly in step with rising earnings. So whilst inflation increases the cost of new building, it reduces the cost of earlier building.

Owner-occupiers, like the government and everyone else, condemn inflation as wholly pernicious, without a redeeming feature. Nevertheless, if they own outright, they watch the value of their investment grow rapidly, and rejoice. For those who are still buying, if they bought some time ago their feelings will be much the same. If they have bought recently the weight of the financial burden they have taken on will be foremost in their thoughts; but they will be comforted by the realisiation that the annual increase in the value of their property will exceed what has to be paid out in mortgage repayments, and that the real cost of those repayments, as in the case of public sector housing, will be falling.

To would-be home-owners, not yet on the home-ownership escalator, things look very different. Rocketing house prices are for them a very serious problem. The amount needed for a deposit and legal and other costs may well be rising faster than they can save.

Central government and housing finance

Governments have always needed to know how much they had to raise by taxation to meet the calls that would be made on them – and this used to be about all they needed to know. In modern times, however, they find themselves attempting to manage the economy, and in this connection they are concerned, among other things, with the share of the total national income which the public sector will absorb. A large part of this sector's needs will be met by taxation and other revenue. The balance is referred to as the Public Sector Borrowing Requirement (PSBR), unheard of a few years ago, today forever on the lips of politicians, economists, and leaders of the financial and business worlds.

Each year, when it has been decided how much the country can afford, and how it should be divided between the main spending departments, a White Paper entitled *The Government's Expenditure Plans* is published. This gives details for each group of services (defence, social security, housing and so on). It sets out for each expenditure during the five previous years, the current year, the coming year, and the following two years.

The purpose is supposed to be to explain the government's intentions and strategy, and relate these to the various services. Before 1977 the information given was unbelievably scanty, virtually useless as a guide to local authorities and others as to what was expected of them. A Committee of the House of Commons took this in hand and as a result there was a vast improvement in 1977 and the two following years; but alas, since 1980 the White Papers have, at least as far as the housing programme is concerned, reverted to their former inadequacies.

The figures for the housing programme for 1986-87, taken from the White Paper (Cmnd 9702, January 1986) are shown on pages 68-69. There are only 11 items for 1985-86 and earlier years; there were 32 for the corresponding years in 1978 and 1979. There is no breakdown whatsoever for the capital part of the programme for 1986-87. For the succeeding two years (not shown here for reasons of space) even this meagre partial analysis is abandoned, and only totals for capital and revenue are given, with no indication as to how these have been arrived at, or how they will be allocated. What use this can be as a guide to those who will have to implement housing policy is not apparent.

The picture which the statement presents is not only inadequate; it is also incorrect and misleading. The capital expenditure total is overstated because of the unexplained omission of loan repayments on council housing – some £455 millions – though repayments on all other borrowings are included.

Worst of all is the way Treasury conventions treat *capital* and *revenue* expenditure. Anyone who buys a house worth say £30,000 with a mortgage for the full amount knows that this will result in expenditure of about £4,000 a year in mortgage repayments.

This will be coupled with financial liability (at first) of £30,000, offset by the ownership of an asset worth £30,000. So far as the householder is concerned, the transaction means that he or she takes on expenditure of

£4,000 a year. This is not how the Treasury sees it. Somehow it manages to persuade itself that there has been expenditure of £34,000 in the first year (£30,000 for the house, £4,000 for the mortgage repayments), and £4,000 a year thereafter.

The consequences of this odd way of seeing things are very serious for a capital intensive operation like housing. It is an easy target for cuts, because the effect will not be felt for some time, so cuts are made and the Treasury claims that they will somehow 'make room' for reductions in taxes, or less government borrowing. This is a travesty of the real position. No council house is built out of government money; it is built out of loans raised (and in due course repaid) by the council. There is no more effect on the government borrowing requirement, or on what will be available for tax reductions, than where money is raised by building societies to finance the purchase of private houses.

The government's Expenditure White Paper published in January 1986 shows how badly housing has fared compared to other spending programmes. Between 1978-79 and 1985-86, while expenditure on law and order went up by 58 per cent in real terms, on social security by 34 per cent and on defence by 30 per cent, the housing programme was reduced by 59 per cent from £6,364 millions to £2,612 millions.

The results for the building programme and for the maintenance of the stock of existing dwellings have been calamitous.

And incredible though it may seem, the biggest element of all in housing finance, the support given by tax relief on mortgage interest, is not even mentioned in the housing programme, though at £4,750 millions in 1985-86, it is more than the total of the entire current and capital expenditure which that programme covers. This irrational way in which central government deals with housing finance is surely in as great a need of reform as the subsidy and tax relief systems themselves.

How it looks to economists

A most valuable contribution to the debate on housing finance came in a paper by two eminent economists, Professors M A King and A B Atkinson, of Birmingham University and the London School of Economics respectively. It was published in the *Midland Bank Review* of May 1980.

They emphasise that the most striking development in housing this

Department of the Environment – housing

£million

	1982-83 outturn	1983-84 outturn	1984-85 outturn	1985-86 estimated outturn	1986-7 plans
Gross capital expenditure					
PUBLIC SECTOR PROVISION					
Renovation of local authority new town stock	966	1,150	1,263	1,130	
New provision for rent:					
by local authorities	736	743	814	620	
by housing associations	769	733	708	683	
by new towns	34	10	18	10	
Total public sector provision	2,504	2,636	2,803	2,443	
SUPPORT TO PRIVATE SECTOR					
Home ownership:					
Local authority and new towns	100	139	106	82	
Housing association low cost ownership	120	140	129	131	
Home loan and option mortgage schemes	4	14	6	3	
Renovation and clearance	573	1,052	870	625	
Total support to private sector	798	1,345	1,111	840	

	1982-83 outturn	1983-84 outturn	1984-85 outturn	1985-86 estimated outturn	1986-7 plans
Gross capital expenditure	3,301	3,981	3,914	3,283	3,253
Capital receipts	− 1,877	− 1,955	− 1,784	− 1,651	− 1,601
Net capital expenditure	1,424	2,026	2,131	1,632	1,652
Current expenditure Subsidies for revenue deficits for local authority, new town and housing association housing	1,101	919	913	948	911
Housing associations and administration	13	14	16	18	23
Local authority administration	113	143	144	144	166
Total current expenditure	1,228	1,076	1,073	1,110	1,100
TOTAL DEPARTMENT OF THE ENVIRONMENT – HOUSING	2,652	3,102	3,204	2,742	2,752

Source: The Government's Expenditure Plans, 1986-87 to 1988-89, Cmnd 9702 II, January 1986

Comment: All the figures are cash, so because of inflation the reduction in the programme figures is much greater in real terms than appears.

The published table shows two preceding years, not given here because of lack of space. It also shows the two years following 1986-87, but only totals for capital and current, and the overall total.

Until this year, exchequer subsidies and rate fund contributions were shown separately. Now there is only one figure (eg £911m for 1986-87) as if they were all government subsidies.

century has been the growth of owner occupation, and that the equity acquired in a house (its value less the outstanding mortgage debt) has come to represent a major component of net wealth.

Their main approach was to compare the two main tenures, public rented and privately owned, by looking at the rate of return on capital which each yields. Taking council housing first, they estimated that the net real rate of return over the previous 10 years had averaged 2.5 per cent, starting at 2.8 per cent in 1968 and falling to around 2 per cent in the years 1974 to 1978. This was lower than in other sectors of the economy, but they saw no reason why this should not be so; housing is a very secure investment, and there are strong social arguments for setting a relatively low rate of return.

For home buyers a number of examples were given, taking varying proportions of mortgage loan to purchase price and varying rates of interest, and allowing for capital gains. They showed that housing costs were typically lower for owner occupiers than they were for council tenants. The cost can in fact be negative, i.e. result in a gain rather than a cost, depending on the rate of tax to which the mortgagor is liable and the rate at which property values increase.

King and Atkinson were in no doubt about the urgent need for reform. They think it is unrealistic to suppose that we can continue with a system of housing finance which is greatly distorted by taxation and inflation, and which leads both to gross inequalities and a bizarre pattern of incentives.

For owner-occupation they favoured the reintroduction of a tax on imputed rental income (the old Schedule A in some form). Although they acknowledged that the proposal is widely regarded as politically unfeasible, they do not accept this. Such a tax is levied in other European countries, and the revenue it would raise would allow offsetting relief in other directions; all that is lacking is political will. Mortgage interest tax relief would continue if Schedule A is reintroduced, so the tax on imputed rental income would be reduced for those who do not own outright; and some special consideration would be needed for retired people on low incomes who are owner occupiers.

Their alternative to a tax on imputed income is to reduce or eliminate tax relief on mortgage interest. One way would be to maintain the then £25,000 mortgage loan ceiling beyond which relief was not available, letting it fall in real terms, so that it would eventually become negligible if inflation persists. This would be the easy option. (But the government has actually *raised* the ceiling to £30,000.)

Another method put forward was to limit relief to a common rate of tax, possibly the basic rate, instead of the present indefensible system which, by giving relief at the highest tax rate for which the mortgagor is liable, gives most help to the wealthiest.

For the public rented sector, the idea of national *rent pooling* needs further consideration as a way of reducing the present variations between different housing authorities. Apart from this, what degree of subsidisation is justified depends on what rate of return is looked for on capital, and this in turn depends on what changes are made to the owner occupied sector. It was possible, according to King and Atkinson, that no increase in council rent levels would be called for, in spite of changes which would increase the cost of housing to owner-occupiers, because tenants were already at such a disadvantage. (Their article was written before the very large council rent increases from 1980 onwards, when rents more than doubled in three years. Tenants are at an even greater disadvantage now.)

As for the *rent rebate* system (now the *housing benefit* system), King and Atkinson rejected means-testing. They preferred some kind of housing allowance not dependent on income, and which included an element related to housing costs.

They stressed repeatedly the need to view the problem as a whole, and while accepting that some housing investment would be deterred if their proposals were adopted, they did not see this as a disadvantage – for one of the drawbacks of present arrangements is the incentive to those on higher tax rates, already well-housed, to over-invest in housing.

Reform: what they say

The need for reform

IT SHOULD BE obvious from what has gone before that the reform of housing finance is urgently needed. Present arrangements result in gross inequities between the different tenures, and within them. They impose a considerable burden on public funds but are singularly ineffective, and therefore wasteful, because of their failure to secure an adequate supply of accommodation, particularly rented accommodation.

In the private sector they do nothing to halt the decline in the number of dwellings available for rent, or in their growing disrepair.

So far as unfitness, disrepair and lack of amenities are concerned, the local authority sector actually has a rather better record than that of owner-occupied housing, and infinitely better than the private rented sector. Yet even here, the Association of Metropolitan Authorities (AMA) has reported the need for spending some £19 billion in England alone; and the government's own survey now confirms the AMA estimate.

As for home ownership, the subsidy given by the taxpayer through tax relief is grotesque in its incidence. It is given automatically, whether there is need or not; it gives most help to the best off. In 1985-86 those with incomes below £5,000 averaged £150 in tax relief, while those with incomes over £30,000 got on average £1,500. £30 help per week for the well-off, £3 a week for the not well-off. Overall, the average was £590, about £11 per week. In the same year, exchequer housing subsidies for council tenants averaged £2 a week.

The volume of savings which are absorbed by the present arrangements must also be a cause for concern. In 1974 there were 9,727,000 owner-occupied dwellings in England and Wales. By 1984 there were 12,424,000, an increase of 28 per cent. But building society advances (which finance the great majority of house purchases) increased by 707 per cent, from £2,920m in 1974 to £23,771m in 1984. Higher prices account for part of this enormous expansion, but most of the money is going on existing houses, as they change hands, and not on providing new ones. A large sum also goes on 'leakage' from the private housing market – the Bank of England estimates some £7 billion in 1984 – as mortgagors, on changing houses, do not apply all the sale proceeds of the former homes to the purchase of their new homes. Clearly, changes of ownership have to be financed, and as prices rise, this costs more; but it is sobering to consider how large a proportion of building society funds have to be devoted to this purpose, compared with the amount going to actual additions to the housing stock. In 1974, one loan in four went on a new dwelling; in 1984 it was one loan in seven.

Present policies make things worse

The present government sees only one housing problem – how to increase the proportion of owner-occupied housing. Its expenditure white paper (Cmnd 9428-II, January 1985) says flatly: 'The main aim of the Government's housing policy is to increase the level of home ownership'. The importance they attach to this issue is difficult to fathom when the shortage of rented accommodation is growing and Britain already has a larger proportion (over 60 per cent) of owner-occupation than any other advanced industrial country in Europe.

However, there can be no doubt about the intention. Reductions in the housing programme have reduced council building in Great Britain to 20,800 dwellings in 1985 – less than a sixth of what it was in 1975. The right to buy scheme has transferred some 750,000 houses from renting to private ownership. The total stock of rented accommodation, public and private, is down by about 850,000 in ten years.

There are fewer houses for the 1.2 million families on council waiting lists, fewer for those seeking transfers, and the annual total of families accepted as homeless has passed the 100,000 mark and is still growing. Large numbers of these have to be put into bed and breakfast accommodation because councils have nothing else to offer them. Bed and breakfast can cost £200 a week or more per family, £10,000 a year, and at the end of it, not a brick laid. The economic folly of all this baffles description.

Another result of present policies to force up rents has been that 70 per cent of tenants cannot pay without help from housing benefits. These rent increases have enabled the government to make 'savings' of £900 millions in housing subsidies, but they appear to have added some £1,200 millions to social security payments. It does not seem to have occurred to the experts that massive rent increases would produce massive increases in benefits for those already claiming, and that they would also add large numbers of new claimants.

Reform again on the agenda

Since 1979 this country's real housing problems have received little notice. The steep rent increases, the virtual phasing out of council house subsidies, the drastic cuts in housing investment, have all met with little opposition. The government has shown no particular interest in the mammoth problems of homelessness, unfitness, disrepair, lack of amenities, and acute housing shortages in many areas.

At last, in 1985, demands for action began to come from all sides. In February Roman Catholic bishops launched a national campaign making all these points, and drawing attention to the 27 per cent increase in a single year – from £2,750m to £3,500m – in the cost of mortgage interest tax relief. 'It is', they said, 'a shock to compare what has been given to those who have homes, and what has been withheld from those who do not.'

In March a leading figure in the building society movement, Tim Melville-Ross of Nationwide, referred to 'our crazy system of housing finance subsidy which favours owner-occupation to the detriment of every other form of tenure', and went on to say that the way to a thorough and radical re-thinking of our housing stock is paved with the abolition of mortgage tax relief.

In April the Royal Institute of British Architects followed up previous calls for action with *Decaying Britain*, an irrefutable case for vastly greater resources and a forceful condemnation of past neglect.

The Royal Institution of Chartered Surveyors came next with a discussion document, *Better Housing for Britain*, analysing all the present shortcomings and calling for heavy investment to increase the housing stock and tackle the enormous problem of disrepair. They estimated an overall shortage of over a million dwellings. Financial arrangements should be changed, they said. Tax relief on mortgage interest should be phased out. There should be a move towards market rents for both private and public rented sectors. Deficits or surpluses on councils' housing accounts should fall on, or accrue to, the Exchequer. Plenty of room for controversy in all this, but good to see the issues so forcefully argued.

The NFHA Report

In July 1985 there was a major contribution from the National Federation of Housing Associations (NFHA), which had set up a committee with a wide range of expertise and interest, chaired by the Duke of Edinburgh. It published its report, *Inquiry into British Housing*, which attracted wide attention, much of it directed to one recommendation, that mortgage interest tax relief was not justified and should be phased out. This is a pity, for this was only one of several equally or more important proposals in the report; and in any case there was nothing startling about it: it is the overwhelming opinion of those concerned with housing finance that it is only political considerations which favour its retention.

The value of the report was actually in its comprehensive survey of the present situation, the arrangements which have produced it, and the challenging solutions it propounds. It recommends a needs-related housing allowance to replace the present jungle of housing subsidies, housing benefits for tenants, mortgage interest tax relief, and the housing element in supplementary benefit. This would put all tenures on the same footing in respect of help with housing costs.

For rents in all sectors a new basis is proposed in the report which would relate rents to current capital values, assuming vacant possession. This would give comparability between all rented dwellings, and while rents would be set to give a reasonable return, they would not be as high as unregulated market rents. A principal advantage of such a system is said to be that rent income could be sufficient to attract private investment, thus reducing the dependence on government subsidy and widening the variety of agencies which would provide rented housing. The report accepts that capital value rents would not be practicable without an adequate housing allowance.

A change in the housing functions of local authorities was also advocated. They would have a greater strategic and co-ordinating role, but they are not seen as the main providers of future rented accommodation.

There were other important recommendations, especially proposals for improving housing conditions. But one of the main objectives of the report was to provide a financial basis which will not have implications for the Public Sector Borrowing Requirement. In other words, the intention was to avoid the need for additional council borrowing, since this, under present Treasury conventions, is treated as if it were government money, though in fact it is nothing of the kind. It was also implied that the present capital grants system for housing associations (which does involve government money), would be replaced by private investment by the financial institutions.

By any standard the NFHA report makes a major contribution to the debate. Some of the principal recommendations, several of them decidedly controversial, will be referred to later.

'Faith in the City'

Finally in December 1985, there came the Report of the Archbishop of Canterbury's Commission on Urban Priority Areas, *Faith in the City*. As its title indicates, its primary concern was the problems of the inner cities, and there are sections on urban policy, poverty and employment, housing, health, social care, education, and order and law. But the analysis, the message, the recommendations, are relevant to our whole society. It is not possible to exaggerate its importance.

Its approach differs materially from that taken by the NFHA inquiry. The latter, whilst stressing the overwhelming need for a great expansion of building to rent, made proposals for reform which were largely shaped by the need, as the members saw it, to operate in the context of present government attitudes. Reform therefore assumed a continuing constraint on borrowing by local authorities, and the need for rents which would attract private investment. Income support subsidies rather than the general housing subsidies of the past were preferred; and an expansion of council provision was not favoured.

Faith in the City, on the other hand, addresses itself to the social considerations on which housing policies should be based, to the principles which should inform the attitudes and actions of government and ourselves. It will be said of it that, unlike the NFHA report, it is lacking in

77

concrete proposals for the finance of housing: and so it is. But its importance lay in its examination of the fundamental deficiencies of existing policies and thinking which have brought us to the present pass. None of the other reports does this, or does it in such depth, yet this must be the first step, not to be avoided if we are to have a rational solution.

Our society, the Churches' Report says, has accepted that every citizen has a right to food, clothing, education and health care adequate to his or her needs, and irrespective of the ability to pay. Yet appropriate housing, which is as fundamental to human development as health care and having enough to eat, has never been accepted as a right for all. Although public rented housing was originally intended, with much success, to break the connection between bad housing and the ability to pay, it has never been funded adequately. Supply has never met demand, and too often council housing has been regarded as 'housing suitable for poor people'. And now that link between poverty and bad housing is being re-established.

Some argue that in any case the public rented sector has failed, and is a product that nobody wants. There is certainly much to be criticised, especially styles of management. Paternalism has flourished. The Labour Party's traditional stance has been that this is a tenure that should be open to all who want it, but the resources have never been available to meet the demand, so there has been allocation on the basis of need, and priority to low income families with children, resulting in unbalanced communities. Maintenance has been scamped from the beginning, tenants have never been involved at any stage, capital costs have been reduced by putting dwellings on cheap inaccessible land and installing central heating systems as cheaply as possible. So the tenants face very expensive transport and fuel costs, and the estates are called 'hard to let' – not 'hard to live in' – as if this was the tenants' fault.

Council tenants – whose average income is less than half that of the average mortgagor – have to bear the cost of caretakers, cleaners, life and grounds maintenance, if they live in high rise accommodation, all unnecessary if they lived at street level, which of course they would prefer. On top of this many tenants pay twice for services such as estate lighting and refuse collection – once in their rates, and again in their rents.

As for the private rented sector, it flourished when costs and interest rates were low, but investment in further provision ceased long ago. The

House of Commons environment committee, reviewing this tenure recently, found that rents must at least double if they are to provide an incentive for the private landlord to invest. But at this level those who could afford to buy would be better off buying; and those forced to rent could only pay if subsidised through a staggering increase in public expenditure on some form of housing benefit. *Faith in the City* saw no future for an expansion of this tenure.

There is the voluntary housing movement. It has made only a small contribution to the total national stock, but has an excellent record in its initiatives and in catering for special needs. It can be a significant force for the future. But at present its financial dependence makes it increasingly subject to government policy.

Present government strategy relies heavily on home ownership. The promotion of this is a deliberate political decision, encouraged directly by government subsidy and indirectly by the withdrawal of subsidy from council housing and pushing up rents. It is claimed that this has opened up choice, and choice is the centre of liberty. But *Faith in the City*'s view was that what characterises the housing conditions of low income people is lack of choice; and whilst owner-occupation does give maximum choice for those who can afford it, and makes good financial sense for them, it will never be available to everyone. The cost of choice for the majority is the absence of choice for the minority who will never be able to buy.

The commission was impressed by some small-scale privatisation schemes of conversion from renting to owner-occupation. But they noted that the improvements needed to attract purchasers were the same as those the tenants want – security; 24 hour caretaking; the conversion of cramped three bedroom flats into spacious homes for single people and childless couples. And Urban Development Grant, available towards the cost of the work if the private sector does it, is not available to the local authority.

In pointing the way forward the commission concluded the housing problem cannot be contained, let alone reversed, without an expanded housing programme. Yet present policies make housing bear the brunt of public expenditure cuts at a time when the decline in private renting is putting ever greater pressure on public renting.

Better standards are needed. A home is more than bricks and mortar, a roof over one's head. Decent housing means a place that is dry, warm, and in reasonable repair. It also means security, privacy, sufficient space, a place where people can grow, make choices, become more whole people. Present standards for public housing are ungenerous in space, and appear to assume that all the household except the wife and young children will be out all day.

Co-operatives should be encouraged; management should be more responsive; maintenance and repair should have higher priority and funding.

Homelessness is a fearsome and rapidly growing problem, and the Homeless Persons Act should be amended so that it covers all the homeless, the report stated. The present categories are totally inadequate as a measure of the need, and should be abandoned.

These things all cost money, but the commission said that if housing were regarded as a priority, money would become available. We are reminded that tax relief for house purchase, being regarded as income foregone rather than expenditure, is not subject to expenditure constraints. Yet it far exceeds the whole of the housing programme, capital and revenue together, in the government's annual public expenditure white paper; and the cost to the community in lost tax revenue in assisting the purchase of a house is more than the cost of providing a home to rent.

Faith in the City reminds us not merely of the size of the physical challenge, and the inequity and inefficiency of present arrangements, but also of the critical importance of decent housing to a just society – in short, of the thinking which should shape the reforms which are so urgently needed.

Reform: the right way ahead

THERE IS NOW a widespread consensus that for many years there has been serious under-investment in housing; that the way we help people with their housing costs is, to say the least, bizarre; and that what has been happening results from our failure to reform our present housing finance arrangements.

But what should rent levels be? How should tenants with low incomes be helped with their housing costs? What of owner-occupation and its costly subsidising through tax relief? What agencies should be responsible for expanding the rented sector, and for administering schemes for repair and improvement of dwellings in all tenures on the scale required?

These are big questions, and there are no easy answers. No consensus has emerged, save as to the magnitude and seriousness of the situation and the growing cost of the reckoning as remedial action is postponed.

Investment

All the things that need doing – building more rented accommodation, eliminating disrepair, modernisation – call for heavy investment. This is the inevitable price for years of neglect, and it cannot be avoided. Delay will only increase the final cost.

The main problem since the 1970s has been on the one hand the need for investment, and on the other a government strategy which sought reductions in public spending and accordingly reduced permission for local authorities to borrow. This, in theory, would lead to lower interest rates, thanks to lower demand for capital. The logic of this is not immediately apparent since the enormous expansion of lending for home-ownership, with its accompanying demand for capital, makes public sector borrowing for housing purposes a trifling, even irrelevant matter, as shown in the table below.

	Total borrowing for capital expenditure on housing – councils, new towns, Housing Corporation		Building society advances for house purchase (UK)
	£m		£m
1974/75	4,829 (GB)	1974	2,920
1978/79	2,176 (England)	1978	8,708
1984/85	2,131 (England)	1984	21,537

The extent of the change defies description. In such circumstances, to argue that the present allocation of borrowing consent for public housing is all that the country can afford calls for a remarkable exercise of faith.

Nevertheless, the NFHA *Inquiry into British Housing*, referred to in chapter 7, assumed for the purpose of its report that present restraints would have to be met by private investment. And it suggested that the financial institutions (pension funds, insurance companies and so on), which certainly could provide the necessary funds, would be prepared to do so by the offer of a 'real' rate of interest of four per cent. By this is meant interest in the first year at four per cent on the amount invested, and in subsequent years four per cent on the original sum increased each year at the rate by which house values have increased. Four per cent on this basis is as attractive as, say, ten per cent on a fixed sum. There is also the increase in the capital sum which investment represents, no small consideration.

This ingenious proposal has its attractions, but there is a serious drawback in the rent levels which it implies, as will be seen later. It would have been better for the NFHA to have grasped the nettle, and pointed out that Treasury attitudes to borrowing are irrational. When a council borrows to build a house, this is not government borrowing. It is a nonsense to treat it as if it were. It has exactly the same effect on the national economy as when a private individual borrows to buy a new house. Both mean the raising of a loan which will in due course be repaid, and both result in an addition to the nation's housing stock.

Councils must have freedom to borrow if their share of the necessary task is to be carried out, and there will have to be some suitable agency –

the Public Works Loan Board or the like – for financing the work to be done by other bodies.

Rents

By 1983 councils were responsible for 71 per cent of rented accommodation, private landlords 23 per cent, and housing associations six per cent.

Economists and other commentators all agree that rents should relate to the size and quality of the dwellings, and that there should be comparability in the rents which tenants pay, irrespective of who the landlord may be. The question still remains as to how the rents should be determined. Virtually everyone accepts that because of acute scarcity, rents cannot be left to market forces.

For councils for over 50 years the idea had been rents which would, as far as possible, cover costs. There were subsidies to meet part of those costs, so that councils could charge rents which were 'reasonable'. But in 1972 the Conservative government applied the 'fair rent' system to council housing, amid some controversy. Labour in 1974 returned to 'reasonable' rents. Conservatives replaced Labour in 1979, and since 1980 rent levels have been whatever the Secretary of State thinks they should be.

From time to time powerful voices have been raised, urging that it is quite wrong that council tenants should benefit from the low historic costs of earlier building; that the only logical basis for rents is a figure that gives a reasonable return on the current value of the landlord's investment; and that there can be no justification for treating landlords any differently from any other investor (though few say leave it on market forces). The proposal is therefore for a reasonable 'real' return on the current value of the property; and year by year, whilst house prices go on rising the return would increase in money terms. This is the formula preferred by the NFHA inquiry.

If we are looking at rented housing with an investor's eye, this is the answer. Because the inquiry attached so much importance to the need to attract private investment, this is indeed the way its members saw the issue.

However, there is a controversial aspect to this 'current capital values' formula. Imagine the outcry if it were suggested that the house-purchaser's costs should rise every year as the value of their property rose. Their costs are geared to what was borrowed when the house was bought; in other words, the purchaser has the benefit of the cost at the time he bought, the historic cost. Yet it is proposed that the housing costs of tenants should be wholly unrelated to the cost of providing the accommodation, should rise every year and, unlike mortgage repayments, should go on forever. There is no social justice in this proposal between those who rent and those who own.

There is another, perhaps even more fundamental, issue. Should the provision of rented housing for that part of the population which on average is substantially less well-off than the owner-occupied sector, now be treated as a commercial proposition, related to house prices which are rising at double the rate of inflation? Or should it be regarded as more in the nature of an essential social service, as it has been in the case of public sector housing for over 60 years?

Housing of an adequate standard is essential to a decent family life and for many other reasons, but it cannot be secured in a society as unequal as ours if commercial considerations have priority.

Besides, it would not work. In the southern half of the country the current (1986) capital value of a three bedroom council house is £40,000. And that means a rent of £40 or more a week, rising every year, even at the four per cent return which the NFHA report suggests.

The only logical solution for the public rented sector, surely, is a rent structure which aims at covering costs, with the help of a much fairer distribution than there is now, of the total financial support – tax relief and subsidies – given to all tenures.

Who will provide the rented accommodation?

Existing provision of housing for rent is by councils, housing associations, private landlords and, to a limited extent, other agencies such as housing co-operatives. Variety of provision is in itself desirable, since it increases freedom of choice for the tenant. So which of the existing providers, or what new agencies, can do what is required?

The private landlord still has admirers. Remove rent controls and, it is argued, market forces will soon reverse the decline of the past 70 years and all will be well. This is a surprising claim, on all past experience, and it will not bear examination.

Housing associations escape the sort of criticism that is directed at the private landlord and at council housing. Nearly all are small, in comparison with the average local authority, and so avoid the appearance of over-large, bureaucratic organisations. Many other countries have used them as the main providers of rented housing; and they have made a valuable contribution in the last ten years in this country. To some who dislike the public sector for ideological reasons they are seen as an admirable expression of the voluntary principle (which they are), and not part of the public sector at all, despite the fact that they depend more on government funding than any other tenure. It seems certain that they will be important in future provision.

Local authorities, however, are under heavy criticism. They are charged with being paternalistic, their management is said to be insensitive and bureaucratic, they have an unsatisfactory record in dealing with repairs, their estates are badly planned, badly maintained, and often lacking in adequate social and shopping facilities. They have shown, it is said, that they are no good as estate managers, and should stick to what they can do. All these charges are true of some councils, but as a general picture, this is a travesty; nevertheless this is how local authorities are widely perceived as landlords.

For these reasons, among others, the NFHA inquiry suggested a new agency, the 'approved landlord', to supplement provision by housing associations. This, it was claimed, could offer real scope for the building societies, some of which accept that the shortage of rented accommodation is a serious problem, and wish to be involved as providers instead of confining themselves solely to financing home-ownership. The pension funds and other institutions would likewise be attracted, provided that they can expect security and a reasonable return. It is assumed that they would not want to be directly involved, except as investors, and would prefer the business of providing the houses, and the subsequent management to be done by separate specialist bodies who would be 'approved' landlords, subject to a code of conduct and to local monitoring. They would charge rents based on current capital values. There would probably be a need for subsidies in the early years.

But the *Inquiry* envisaged only a limited role as providers for local authorities. Their unpopularity as landlords and their unsatisfactory track record are seen as precluding them from any main responsibility in this field. Instead, their main future task, in addition to bringing their existing stock up to a suitable standard, should be in a strategic sphere. This would include co-ordination and research, the enforcing of standards in all sectors, and the provision of agency services to help with improvement and repair in the owner-occupied sector.

The NFHA inquiry does valuable service in discussing this issue in depth, and making proposals for new initiatives. Yet to many people concerned with housing, many of the judgments on local authorities as landlords will be controversial and not sufficiently supported by past experience. The inquiry seems to accept too readily their alleged inadequacies, and to ignore the reasons for them, especially the crippling effects of central government restraints on capital and revenue spending. There is bureaucracy and poor tenant/landlord relationships in many areas. But the very success of councils as providers had already made them large-scale landlords by 1973, at which point local government re-organisation made them two or three times as large again by mergers. The danger of bureaucracy with such vast estate management responsi-bilities – there is nothing remotely comparable in any other sector – should have been self-evident.

Yet reform is already under way among progressive councils. They are introducing area management, genuine tenant involvement, and better repairs' services, with no visible encouragement from central govern-ment. And the inquiry seems to have overlooked that councils are at least accountable, much more so than housing associations, whilst private landlords are not accountable at all.

There are also certain vital practical considerations if rapid large-scale provision is to be secured. In every area in the country there is an already existing housing authority – the local council – for which a management structure exists and for which there are maintenance facilities by the landlord's own workforce, supplemented as necessary by private con-tractors. The authority will have a fund of experience in the provision of new dwellings. It will have an already existing stock of rented accommo-dation, much of it built in earlier years at costs far below today's, which will be of inestimable benefit from the financial point of view. There will also be in the council the facilities for raising capital and managing the loan debt. And waiting to be tapped, there is the potential for national pooling which, by applying the principles already in operation in each housing area individually, could lessen the cost anomalies that now exist between the more fortunate and less fortunate areas.

No other agency has these immense advantages. And whilst it is true that the greater the variety of agencies which can be harnessed to the task of expanding the rented stock, the better, to assume that the local authorities will not have a leading part to play is quite unrealistic.

Subsidies

For practical purposes there are two kinds of subsidy – housing subsidies and income support subsidies. Housing subsidies are payments or other financial support which reduce the cost of housing generally, without regard to the circumstances of the individual. Council house subsidies, capital grants to housing associations, and tax relief on mortgage interest are such subsidies. There are no housing subsidies to private landlords.

Income support subsidies are those which apply to the individual householder, taking account of circumstances and ability to pay. Housing benefits and supplementary benefit payments by the DHSS to help low income mortgagors, are this kind of subsidy.

The expression 'subsidies to people rather than to bricks and mortar' is much in vogue at present. The argument is that housing subsidies, whether they take the form of payments from the exchequer to housing authorities or tax relief to mortgagors, are wrong in principle because they do not take individual circumstances into account. They therefore give help to some who do not need it. So instead of housing subsidies which reduce housing costs generally, together with housing benefits which further reduce the cost for those with low incomes – as at present – there should only be the latter.

The NFHA inquiry took this view. All housing subsidies, including tax relief, should be phased out. This would mean that the housing costs of council tenants and mortgagors would be higher; but the householders, whatever the tenure, would be protected if their circumstances required it by what the inquiry called a 'needs related housing allowance' (in other words a housing benefit of some kind).

At first sight this NFHA proposal has a great deal to recommend it. It would clear away the present jungle of schemes; it would be easily understood; and it could be so designed that the objectionable means-test features of the existing housing benefits scheme are avoided. These are no small advantages.

There are, however, some problems. Even in 1980 before the recent steep rent increases, about 45 per cent of council tenants were unable to pay their rents without the help of rent rebates or supplementary benefits. The proportion is now 70 per cent. If rents are to be increased further, as is inevitable if there is to be more building but no housing subsidies, then even more tenants, council or private, will be unable to pay their rents without still more help.

And if rents, instead of merely covering costs, are to be based on the current capital value of the dwelling they will be higher still; as will the bill for housing benefits in some form.

The question arises: can there be any logic in rent levels which few, if any, tenants will be able to pay? For that, unfortunately, seems to be the unavoidable result of unsubsidised rents. Subsidies for rented housing are inescapable, and are certainly a lesser evil than no subsidies if this means rents which have no relationship whatsoever to the rent paying capacity of those living in the houses.

Housing subsidies for owner-occupiers

Owner-occupiers benefit from exemption from tax on the rental value of dwellings, and exemption from capital gains tax. But to the public the most important support for home-ownership is mortgage tax relief. The very heavy cost (£4,750 million in 1985-86); its regressive nature (most help to the better-off, least to the worst-off); and the fact that by far the greater part of it goes on existing houses, only a small proportion on new houses, all this is now universally recognised. All that stands in the way of reform is that 60 per cent of all householders are owner-occupiers, and owner-occupiers have votes.

Yet the enormous and rapidly growing cost of this subsidy and its glaring defects mean that reform must come, sooner or later. Leaders of political parties may be at last becoming aware of the difficulty of arguing that the country cannot afford to put extra resources into new building and more repair and improvement, when such huge existing commitments produce so little.

When they consider what they might do about tax relief, the following considerations will present themselves:

1 Any change must be phased, because so many commitments have been entered into on the assumption that present arrangements will continue.

2 Few votes would be lost by immediate discontinuance of relief at marginal tax rates. Who can justify relief at 60 per cent for a rich person and 29 per cent for a poor person?

3 Small successive reductions in the mortgage ceiling figure (now £30,000) eligible for relief, with the new ceiling applying to future mortgages. There would be no effect on existing borrowers, but over a period the saving to the exchequer would be considerable.

4 The Housing Centre Trust suggested some years ago what it called the 'single annuity' system whereby a mortgagor would be entitled to relief for the life of a mortgage, but not thereafter. The proposal never received the attention it deserved, and needs looking at again.

5 Interest rates vary frequently and quite widely. Between 1978 and 1985 there have been eighteen changes, with mortgage interest rates fluctuating between 8½ and 15 per cent. The time for change is when interest rates are falling.

Changes, clearly, can be made. There has been no hesitation about overturning wholesale the support arrangements for tenants – not that this brutal approach has any merit. Whether it concerns mortgagors or tenants, change should be gradual.

Income support subsidies

There will be a continuing need for help by some form of income support. If there are housing subsidies, income support will not be needed by so many, or to the same extent. But it will still be needed.

Whatever happens the present bureaucratic nightmare of housing benefits, with its offensive means-test provisions, must be replaced. Other countries hear with astonishment of this British system which calls for a detailed catechism of each applicant though all the relevant information is already, or should be, in the hands of the local authority and the Inland Revenue. It is as if the use of computers had not yet reached these shores.

There are advocates of a housing allowance which would not be needs-related at all, but paid as of right to all householders, like child benefits or old age pensions, with the tax system amended so that the exchequer will recover the cost where the allowance is not needed. This seems to have considerable merits and warrants careful examination.

Whatever the system of income support, no part of the cost should fall on the locality. It should be borne by the community at large, through an income support subsidy from the exchequer.

Can it be done?

It is odd that it should have taken so long for the seriousness of the housing crisis to be widely recognised; but at last there is movement.

There are two main issues: first, the financial and other arrangements which determine what resources will be available for housing – to what extent, and how, the housing costs of householders in different tenures should be assisted out of public funds; what agencies are best suited for providing and administering rented housing. Secondly, and equally important, the physical task of providing more housing where it is needed and making good the neglect of decades in the maintenance and upgrading of existing stock.

The government's attention still appears to be focused solely on the need, as it sees it, to increase the number of owner-occupiers – though this is the least of our problems. Everyone else is now aware of the scandalous increase in homelessness, the huge problem of disrepair, the waiting lists, the link between deprivation and bad housing conditions in the inner cities and the recent violent disturbances there.

The enormous cost of the tax privileges which benefit owner-occupation but achieve so little is now continually stressed, when not long ago it was almost indecent to mention it.

And with all this everyone sees the apparently uncontrollable house price explosion in much of the country which puts home ownership still further out of reach for young couples and families on waiting lists. The acute scarcity of rented accommodation which denies choice is recognised as one of the main factors which is driving house prices upwards. Mobility is seriously affected, exhortations to those looking for a job that they should move to more favourable areas are a mockery. The great divide between north and south, between those who own and those who cannot afford to own, grows steadily wider.

But change is in the air. There is another development, at first sight quite separate from housing problems, which is that unemployment has become a vital political issue for which remedies must be found. And the biggest single contribution to a reversal of the upward trend of unemployment is staring the political leaders in the face – a resolute attack on the housing problem.

In spite of all the need that has been catalogued earlier, there are some 400,000 unemployed building workers, and it has been estimated that they cost the country £6,000 a year per person in social security and lost tax revenues: £2,400 millions a year. Yet building houses is labour intensive, repairing or modernising them even more so, and virtually all the materials needed except the timber are home produced.

The building trade is in the doldrums, working to a fraction of its capacity. Little danger there of excess demand producing inflationary pressure. Putting the industry to work should have absolute priority, from every point of view, and that work will at the same time be increasing the national wealth by creating long life assets of steadily growing value.

It can be done. And the two reports discussed above have shown us the economic and social folly of recent years, and in large measure pointed the way we need to go.

Index

Page references in bold type correspond to where a definition is given in the text

Annuity mortgages	3, **53**
Better housing for Britain	75
Capital expenditure	**3**, 9, 11, 66, 67, (table 68/9) (table 82)
Capital gains tax	**59**, 70, 88
Capital receipts	**3**, (table 68/9)
Prescribed proportions of,	5, **6**, 11, 23, 24
Certificated housing benefit	**44**, 46
Composite tax rate	**52**
Council housing	
Rate of return on,	**70**
Subsidies for,	**12**, 13, 14, 15, 16
Sale of,	**19**, 20, 21, 22, 23
Decaying Britain	75
Deficiency subsidy	**12**, 13, 14, 15
Endowment mortgages	**53**, 54
Fair rents	**33**, 34, 36, 38, 40
Faith in the City	77, 78, 79, 80
Grant redemption fund	**28**
Housing Act 1980	
Subsidies under,	7, 10, **15**, 58, 64
Housing Association grant	**26**, 27, 64

Housing Benefit
  Government subsidies for,   **11**, 26, 79
  Changes under Social Security Act 1986,   45, **46**
Housing benefit supplement   **45**
Housing capital account   3
Housing Finance Act 1972   **13**, 34
Housing Investment Programme   **5**, 14, 23, 24
Housing repairs account   **9**
Housing revenue account   **7**, 8, 9, 10, 11, 12,
                                     22, 23, 63, 64

Inquiry into British Housing   76, 82, 83, 84, 85,
                                     86, 87, 88

Loan charges   **3**, 9, 13, 17, 63,
                                     65
Loans fund   **4**, 20, 55

MIRAS (Mortgage Interest Relief At Source)   **58**
Mortgage tax relief   2, 47, **55**, 56, 57,
                                     59, 62, 64, 67, 70,
                                     73, 75, 76, 80, 81,
                                     87, 88, 90

Needs allowance   **42**, 43, 44, 47

Option mortgage subsidy   **58** (table 68/9)

Paying for local government   6
Public Expenditure   66
  Housing programme,   **66**, 67

Rate fund contributions   **7**, **11**
Rate support grant   **16**, 17
Rents
  General principles,   **83**
  Controlled,   32

Index

Rent allowances	40, 28, 29, 35, 50
Rent control	**32**, 33, 34, 62
Rent pooling	**17**, 18, 71
Rent rebates	10, 28, **39**, 40, 44, 71
Revenue deficit subsidy	**27** (table 68/9)
Revenue expenditure	**7**, 66, 67
Right to buy	10, **19**, 20, 21, 22, 54, 74
Rising costs subsidy (see also deficiency subsidy)	**13**
Schedule A tax	**56**, 57, 70
Shorthold Tenancies	**35**, 36
Single annuity system	**89**
Sinking fund method	**3**
Standard housing benefit	**42**, 43, 44, 46
Subsidies	10, 11, 12, 13, 14, 15, 16, 17, 18, 26, 38, **39**, 71, 75, 76, 77, 79, 83, 87, 88, (table 68/9)
Variable interest arrangements	**50**, 53

Other Shelter publications you will want to buy

Home Ownership
A suitable case for reform

by MICHAEL BALL

AT A TIME when housing policy seems to revolve exclusively round promoting home ownership at any price, Michael Ball's new book argues that the tenure is in the grip of a major crisis. High levels of mortgage debt, a deteriorating housing stock and low levels of housebuilding, combined with increasing mortgage defaults and ever-rising house prices are symptoms of this crisis.

☐ Michael Ball argues that this crisis is rooted in the current institutional structure of home ownership provision. If this structure is not drastically reformed, the next few years could spell disaster.

☐ The book proposes a 10 point programme of reform, including controlled house prices and housebuilding organised to meet local needs by publicly accountable non-profit bodies.

☐ "A radical restructuring of owner occupation on the lines proposed might seem a tall order" concludes Michael Ball, "but the extent of the current structural crisis, and the almost zero effect of more limited reforms, make it essential".

£3.95 from Shelter Publications (157, Waterloo Road, London SE1 8XF. Cheques payable to Shelter.) Only £2.95 to Shelter members.

Filling the Empties
Short Life Housing and How To Do It
by ROSS FRASER of the
Empty Property Unit

ALREADY dubbed the "short life bible", this exciting new book is the first comprehensive how-to-do-it guide to short life housing – the temporary use of empty property for homeless people. It covers:
* Setting up a short life housing cooperative * Negotiating for houses * Short life lettings and the law * Obtaining funding * How to meet statutory housing standards * Allocations and equal opportunities * Moving on to permanent housing * The dangers of asbestos *

This 192 page book is technical without ever being dull, well illustrated, and is an essential resource for **local authorities** looking for alternatives to bed and breakfast hotels; **housing associations** seeking to extend their activity with temporary housing schemes; **short life housing groups** seeking to improve their service; and **homeless people** hoping to set up housing cooperatives to meet their housing needs.

Copies are available from SHELTER, 157 Waterloo Road, London SE1 8XF at £5.95 (post free – money with orders please). **For Shelter members the price is £4.95** (post free). An extra discount is available for orders of five or more copies of £4.95 each (non-members) or £3.95 each (Shelter members).

Join the campaign!

Were you a member of Shelter when you bought this book! If so, you would have had a £1 discount. Similarly, with all of Shelter's new books. Membership of Shelter offers you more besides...a free quarterly campaign newspaper, regular briefing papers from Shelter's research department on what's new in housing, massive discounts on Shelter's annual conference, and the opportunity to participate in the campaign for the homeless through campaign forums and electing Shelter's board members.

All this for £7.50 if you join as an individual (£3.00 unwaged); voluntary organisations pay £15 and other organisations pay £25.

For details write to:
Membership Secretary,
Shelter,
157 Waterloo Road,
London SE1 8XF.